THE CHILDREN OF R:

Bril

THE CHILDREN OF R:

"Plans from Beyond the Earth Plane"

I.3.0.

Ranald

Published by:
Taijitu House Publishing Co.

1.3.0. (Ranald)
The Children of R:
Plans From Beyond the Earth Plane
www.TaijituHouse.com

ISBN-13: 978-0692394649 (Taijitu House)

Taijitu House
www.TaijituHouse.com
taijituhouse@gmail.com

First Edition
U.S.A

TAIJITU HOUSE
Powerful Books for Enlightened Minds

About the Author

Ranald or simply known as 1.3.0. , (pronounced one, three, zero,) is a Chime; one of a trinity of spirits that incarnated here to Earth with the mission to share a message from The Council in Aldebaran. Aldebaran is a multi-planet Star System located in the Taurus Constellation; more specifically, "The Bulls-Eye." The Council in Aldebaran is responsible for this sector of our Galaxy administered by the Galactic Council.

During his Earth life, Ranald was a Nuclear Engineer in the U.S. Army - he was granted high level security clearances which enabled him to work in Operation Gladio B and a little known esoteric arm of the U.S. Government. Additionally Ranald is a 32nd Degree Freemason and a member of the Scottish Rite.

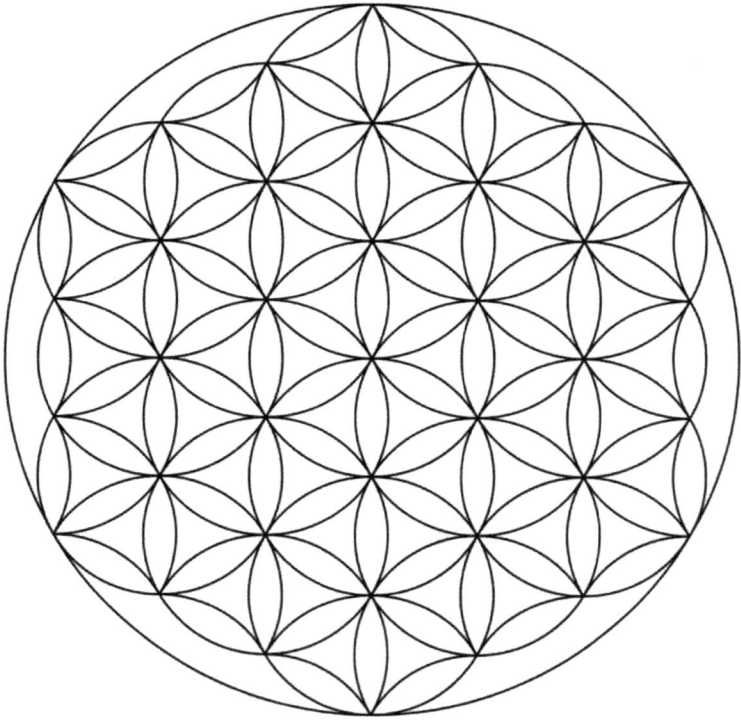

Note from the Publisher

The author is 100% literal with the information presented in this book; he has been verified as a retired veteran of the U.S. Army retiring at the paygrade of E6. We were provided video footage, pictures, documentation, and ID cards both for military service and Freemasonry. This further verified his story and that he is a 32nd Degree Free and Accepted Mason.

Additionally the other two "Chime" who are mentioned in later chapters have also been verified as previously living people. On record we have photographs of all three Chime and have spoken with a third party who verified mutual experiences.

Based on the information that we have gathered, Ranald was not alone in his belief of whom and what he is. So please read this book with the understanding that this document is written as a true story and not a work of science fiction. However, ultimately, it is up to you to decide what you choose to believe or disbelieve.

Publisher's Mission

It is Taijitu House's mission to flex and expand the minds of our readers in order to help humanity develop a broader perspective of ourselves, the Earth, our solar system, the planets, galaxy, the Universe, and the role that we play as individual microcosms existing within this macrocosm. However we do not hold the ideas, beliefs, and opinions of our respected authors.

Reality is an infinite creation with unlimited potential, possibilities, probabilities, and likelihoods. It truly is infinite...

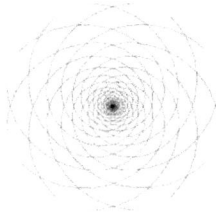

✠ Contents

foreword:

How This Book Came to Be

foreword: How this Book Came to Be

By A.J. Christoph
Taijitu House, Founder

I was first introduced to 1.3.0 almost a year ago while visiting a friend. My plan was to ask for their assistance in promoting my book, *The Book of Powers: Practices for Unleashing Your Full Potential.* However fate had a different plan, instead I was asked to help publish this book, *The Children of R.*

My friend informed me they were assisting someone in publishing a channeled document titled *The Children of R,* and asked if I was interested in adding a new title to my newly formed publishing company. I asked if the author was interested in my assistance then please have him call me. Sure enough a few days later I received the call. He introduced himself by his given Earth-born name. We chatted for about an hour. I was very interested in meeting him. So we scheduled a meeting. It was during our first meeting when things began to become; interesting to say the least...

Per his request it was decided that we would publish this book under a pseudonym. He only wanted to be known as 1.3.0. , but I suggested for search engine reasons that he create a penname in addition to 1.3.0. He agreed and gave me the name "Ranald."

During our first meeting I saw 1.3.0. was just an average ordinary man, at first there was nothing in particular about him. He is of normal height, weight, drives an ordinary car, and appears to just be a typical 50 some year old "good ole' country boy." Except that when we were able to speak in private and away from others, the things that he had to share were quite extraordinary, unbelievable, exciting, and at times even too much for me to handle.

There was always an eerie ounce of truth behind what he spoke about, not only with his ability to describe reality in such a technical and scientific manner, but also in the way that he had a thorough and credible answer for any question I asked. When I would question him there was never a delay, his responses were immediate and without any hesitation. He appeared to truly have information that was "from beyond the earth plane", but at this point I was still skeptical and unsure as to what to think about him. So I just continued to listen and ask questions.

He has a mysterious energy about him; in one sense he is like a child with the purity of his intentions and the ability to speak unrestricted. In another way, he is like Buddha with memories of lifetimes and experiences of entire galaxies that cannot be explained in any rational manner.

No matter how deep of a question I asked, he always had an answer of astronomical understanding. For example we were sitting there at a restaurant and he began drawing a map of our galaxy and our specific location within it. He further explained the various types of beings that occupy various sectors of our galaxy, and how right now there is a galactic war going on and Earth just happens to fall on the edges-between the areas controlled by the opposing forces.

When I asked him how he knew all of these things, he explained it as: "learning to increase your volume."

I remember at our second or third meeting we were having lunch at a country dinner; he was talking about the esoteric technique of how to "step around the corner". This is a technique that he used in the military to "locate" things. He asked if I had ever seen the movie "*The Men Who Stare at Goats.*"

I told him yes, I had watched it while I was deployed to Iraq. He said this was a real program and it continues today, he was a part of one of its "wings". These practices are used to quite literally "step around the corner. Out of your body and to which ever location you desire," and among other things such as locating subjects of interest, and as a method of offense. He added these things are placed in certain movies as a method to combat the enemy, however, the majority of the film and music industry are totally controlled by what he will later define as the "Dominion".

Some good examples of films that were inspired by "Chime", are Avatar, The Matrix, The Men Who Stare at Goats, and others. "Dominion" controlled films and music are not hard to miss. How does the movie or music make you "feel?" What is its purpose? Is it evil?

The same day I noticed he was wearing a peculiar sterling silver stone ring. When I asked him about the ring he showed me that it swiveled around to display the 32nd Degree Freemason symbol, a centered "G" with a compass and square. This opened conversation up further and we spoke about many of the tests, rituals and the history of Freemasonry and its relation to the Knights Templar. However he did make it clear that he was not to share anything that was inappropriate for me to hear. He added that a man is nothing without his word.

In order to add further credibility to the things he was telling me and to help me understand the seriousness of this message; he showed me his various forms of identification both for Freemasonry and the military. Including a Veteran Affairs identification card, a retired U.S Army ID (his paygrade E6 was listed.) Then he revealed a few forms of identification that I was unaware even existed; the identification cards of Freemasonry. He had three separate Freemasonry cards that displayed his degree, that he was an active member of the Scottish Rite, and among other things that I did not fully understand. These ID cards are similar to the military ID cards that I had, meaning that they are advanced with microcomputer processors. This surprised me because it helped place in perspective how extensive of an organization Freemasonry is. I am not a Freemason so I was unaware.

After I finished my meal he invited me to visit what he called a "Vortex." This Vortex is an upwards flowing channel of energy that quite literally can make water flow up hill; it is located at a spring where water comes up out of the ground. Here he said this energy can be used to cleanse you, carry away your negativity and pick up the finished product at another location. The Vortex starts at around 50,000 feet above the Earth's surface and slowly comes down, through the Earth, to the core, and it comes back out at another location. The process takes approximately 4 hours. The location that we visited was the up side. He said if I hang out here enough I will see UFO's among other strange things.

On my third or fourth visit to this location during the recent snow storm in February 2015, I brought a friend along. The wind was blowing hard, snow was coming, trees were falling, and it wasn't a good time to be out driving around, but something in my mind told me we needed to go regardless. So we continued, just my friend and I. Immediately after arriving to the spot where 1.3.0 showed me, I looked up and saw a UFO. I was uncertain what it was, it could have been the ISS, a satellite, or anything else, but it certainly was in orbit. My friend claimed to see it move in a curved trajectory. I didn't catch that part, but my friend believes it was definitely not just a satellite. The wind was picking up and the storm was coming on hard by this point. So we came and saw what we were supposed to see. So quickly we left. A little amazed, we got out of there.

Another day 1.3.0 invited me to visit his Freemason "Blue Lodge" where he earned his third degree, Master Mason. This was my first time entering a Freemason Lodge, which was something I had thought of in the past, but had yet to experience. The time was now.

When we arrived at his lodge he unlocked the door and we proceeded inside, no one else was there, just he and I. He gave me a quick tour and explained many of Freemasonry's symbols and history. I was surprised to find a globe of the Earth and a Celestial Globe sitting on two columns, the celestial map was a spherical globe with all of the constellations from Earth's perspective. These items were said to be very old, dated pre civil war. During the Civil War he said Freemason brothers would still come together to do their duties regardless of which side of the war they were on. Interesting I thought.

After we left the lodge I filmed an interview with him sitting outside on the lodge's steps. But I am uncertain of whether the video should be released as of yet.

Over this past year I have had the opportunity to get to know Ranald fairly well. Fairly well, considering that he is a man with many identities and countless layers of being, so I am not sure if anyone really knows who he is in his entirety. However with all of these interesting experiences and our long talks I feel secure in vouching for his moral character and the credibility that he does have true secrets to reveal, how he got them all, I cannot vouch for 100%, considering I do not know.

As extraordinary as it may sound, this manuscript, *The Children of R,* was directly communicated to 1.3.0. by the authority of "The Council in Aldebaran"; in hopes of assisting us Earthlings to join The Galactic Council and enter into an interstellar age.

So I suppose you could say 1.3.0. "Chimed" in to share this message because The Council believes Earth/humanity is about ready.

foreword Continued:
"Battle Plans for Earth"

What is This Book's Purpose?

This book serves three main purposes, the first purpose is to share the message of The Council to all human being waveforms here on Earth, the second purpose is to expand human consciousness to accept that we are not alone in this infinite Universe, and the final and perhaps the most important purpose is to help humans understand the importance of self-clearing their negative karma and offer additional keys to free humanity from the control of the manipulators.

This text expands our understanding to help humans see that evil isn't something quite as simple as just one force, one being, or one spirit. Additionally this book will help the reader see "how deep the rabbit hole goes", how far the controllers have rooted themselves into our society, and how their programs are degrading the purity of this world, the human Life-Wave, and how if we do not do something about it, we will be destined for another cataclysm, another annihilation similar to the ancient destruction stories such as Sodom and Gomorrah and the flood stories of the various Ancient Texts. According to 1.3.0. previous worlds and civilizations have been destroyed, wiped out, and cleansed from this planet and from other planets across the Galaxy. Destruction is always an opportunity for renewal, an opportunity to create a world that is not susceptible to the influence of the Dominion. He says, "The Aldebarans have done so, and they are urging us to do so as well. That is if we wish to continue to survive as a species or even as a planet or solar system."

"The Ark is coming and we don't have much time to prepare."

I also want to make this clear; our intentions are not to induce panic, spread fear, conspiracies or to make people paranoid. Paranoia is not healthy. So please don't be paranoid. Instead this book should be viewed as a source of motivation and inspiration for all of humanity, and if we can get the message, then we have no reason to be afraid. Even 1.3.0. himself is not afraid; he knows his mission is nearing completion. It is death that gives value to life. But he urges us; we need to understand this message; to evolve beyond the programming of greed, selfishness, manipulation, domination, propaganda, violence and control.

Humans need to return to a pure state free of corruption, impurity, pollution, and strive to consciously banish all of the Dominion's control out of our existence, out of our world, and most importantly out of our individual minds. If all humans can do this then:

"The battle will have been won."

As a final closing note before I introduce 1.3.0 and The Council's message; I want to make it clear that I initially thought the author was just speaking in metaphors and riddles of astronomical proportion, but now I see that his story is far beyond anything that can just be simplified as a fairy tale.

Thank you for taking the time to read this introduction. May this book enlighten and expand all of human consciousness, awareness, perception, compassion and understanding.

Sincerely,

A.J. Christoph
Taijitu House, Founder
2/17/2015

THE CHILDREN OF R:

Vril

1.3.0.

"Plans from Beyond the Earth Plane"

1.3.0

Introduction:
"Plans From Beyond the Earth Plane"

Greetings friends, I wish to convey to you the love and friendship from the Council of Aldebaran. This book is to present material to you from another solar system and we will with some hope, welcome your society into the Galactic Council. Please know that I was assigned this task and I intend to fulfill this in my highest and best form, and convey the messages in the best way possible. The book includes some names of races of beings that I am sure you do not know exists. I want you to understand these names are chosen to represent the various groups are translated in the best way to convey the meaning in the native tongue for each one. However I do realize that these names may be similar to names you know from Earth groups but there is no connection. As an example, I will introduce the inhabitants of what I refer to as Aldebaran. Here, this term Aldebaran refers to a star in the constellation Taurus. Actually from Earth's view this is pretty close, in location but the location I refer to is actually a planet, much larger than Earth. This planet harbors two distinct races of beings. One is very much human like in appearance, and I will call them the Aldebaran's, and the other is similar to what you might call "Ascended Masters" who are called Chime. Both of these races live and die, except both live much longer than Earth people. Both of these races have a representative government called The Council on Aldebaran.

The Aldebaran Council was tasked by the Galactic Council to aid Earth Humans in the struggle against an enemy which they have no experience. The Aldebaran Council sent Chime to perform this task. Please note that Earth is a small and insignificant place which has wound up in a battle zone in the Galaxy. There are many similar places and the Galactic Council appointed a member society to them as well. Please be sure to understand that Aldebaran Chime and Aldebaran Humanoids may be present on Earth at any time, none are allowed to ally with any particular religion or government. Any such activity should point you directly to the opposing group. The Council wants to express no Chime nor Aldebaran Humanoid is an angel or characters of legend in any earth religion.

The next group that I would like to describe is "The Administrators", and this group is not like anything I have heard of here, in any system, religion or other belief. These are a race of all powerful beings that predate the formation of the matter world and have complete and unimpeded control of it. "The Administrators" are basically assigned to look after all of the matter and anti-matter worlds in all dimensions. I want to point out that "The Administrators" are not angels or any other being in any Earth legend or system. Earth people cannot come into contact with them in any way, nor can the human like Aldebaran people. Only Chime can interact with "The Administrators." The only other interaction I know of where "The Administrators" have come into direct influence of the humans is via entering into an illusion of interspace travel, when actually those humans went nowhere; this was done to facilitate a situation which arose with the next group. It is not important to almost all humans, in any case. The last group I will mention is the "Dominion", I have tried to provide a less used term for them but pretty much

"Dominion" is what they call themselves. Historical documents in The Council at Aldebaran call them at times, the Slaveholders, the Conquers and the Evil Event Makers. Perhaps they have used similar names in the past here on Earth, if so I am not certain, but it remains possible. In any case the

Introduction:
"Plans from Beyond the Earth Plane"

Dominion are not demons, fallen angels, devils or evil spirits, although some may resemble such descriptions in part. The Aldebaran Chime sent to aid Earth in this conflict, have made little headway in Human affairs and this book was the last great directive to reaching out to Earth Humans. Also decades ago a decision was made to fill these positions with Earth Humanoids and allow the Chime to return to Aldebaran and Earth to seal its own destiny. The Chime has played a significant and very behind the scenes role and the time is drawing to an end. Chime are not your legendary beings and always referred to themselves through the ages on Earth as initially the "Children of R" which is technically correct for all Aldebaran's. (R is the word for the Creator on Aldebaran).

Also used on Earth was; Beings of an Inner Light, Self- Illuminated Ones, Illumina, and the last term as "The Shining Ones." All of these terms were basically stolen by the Dominion along the way, and began to be used by Dominion influenced opposing groups as well to cast a suspicion or fear upon us, so the reaction of The Council was that the names were changed. I will use the term, "The Children of R," but please note this has no connection to any other system on Earth using the same or similar term. To say "Oh, I have heard of them" is incorrect at best.

I also want to inform the reader that the book conforms to the wishes of The Council and therefore must contain facts with no bias. The Council is very strict on this matter. Again I must inform you that I am the Chime known on Aldebaran as Chime 130 (One Three Zero, my creation appearance number, and all Chime are named this way.) Chime live in a sort of cluster of three and mine has two others living here alongside me, (in non-corporeal form) and when we are done here, Earth will have Earth Human born "Earth 33", only. My Chime group fought in the battle to defend Aldebaran over 50 thousand years ago, your time is upon you soon. We have seen what the deception of greed, lust for power and all variety of wicked behavior brings. Aldebaran lost the largest majority of its population, to include all of the "Dominion" collaborators, during this struggle. I wish you all the best in your Endeavor against the deviousness and deception of the "Dominion."

You will need it.

With all the Love that a Chime can convey,

1.3.0.

Chapter 1:
Maria Ortisch and the Vril

Vril

Chapter 1:
Maria Ortisch and the Vril

Maria Ortisch is a medium who was one of the founders of the Vril Society, Vril Gesellschaft or perhaps more correctly stated the Alldetsche Gesellschaft für Metaphysik. She was from Zagreb, Croatia and had a German Mother and a Croat father. She moved to Germany sometime after WWI into the Munich area. She conducted medium work for a few groups which represented the German unity at the time. She had at least two other women who worked with her at the time one named Traute, and one other was referred to as Sigrun (a name given to one of the Norse legend Wotan's daughters). The women used a method of divination called Makarra which made use of extremely long ladies hair, a specially designed scrying board, and a black stone. At this time the medium work was being done for an organization called Thule Gesellschaft or Thule society led by Rudolf von Sebottendorf and Dietrich Eckart. Maria disappeared after the end of WWII. Now she is the new Head of the Council of Aldebaran. Maria was selected because she was an earth Waveform, and can be on the same wavelength as Earth people. I will not discuss any detail of Maria's last days in Germany or post war detail, in accord with her personal privacy, which she has requested. The other

Chapter 1:

Maria Ortisch and the Vril

ladies in the Vril Society went on post war to either
disappear, or to become teachers to the other "The
Children of R." One of these ladies was my mentor.

Maria Ortisch and the Makaara board she used
for Divination by placing the black stone in a
nest of her hair and focused on the board.

Chapter 1: Maria Ortisch and the Vril

Maria   Traute   Sigrun   Gudrun   Heike

Einige der wichtigsten "Vril-Damen" zwischen 1922 und 1945

Chapter 1:   Maria Ortisch and the Vril Ladies

Illustration of Vril Lady

Sigrun

Maria and Heike

The pair compromised by Maria and Sigrun channeled a set of texts in the ancient Sumerian dialect, and some in a script known to German Templars which informed them of the original Aryan race. Additionally channeled was the journey from their home world (Aldebaran) to Earth, and various religious and other documentation, and finally a method of manufacturing an Aldebaran type of flying vessel.

A form of energy was given called Vr IL (which is actually two words which mean word for word God Like) now called Vril. Some of the documentation tells of other planets which were aided in this way, and that Aldebaran which had become uninhabitable due to solar activity, had refined them into a new type of state of being. Often the voice channeled from Maria and Sigrun called itself "Sumi" who was the current leader of The Council at Aldebaran.

Dr. W.O. Schumann, a scientist took the information and was able to develop a plan for such a device.

Dr. Winfried Otto Schumann
[1888-1974]

Dr. Schumann was the German Physicist who was first responsible for developing the Vril channelled designs into a functional craft.

The Bell [Die Glocke]

The emerging government system in Germany was undergoing many changes and the prototypes made for research showed promise. The project was undertaken by Germans as the Antriebstechnische Werkstätten or "Vril

Propulsion Experimental Lab". Crafts were built and tested. The Bell is one of these tested craft.

Die Glocke
(The Bell)

Die Glocke

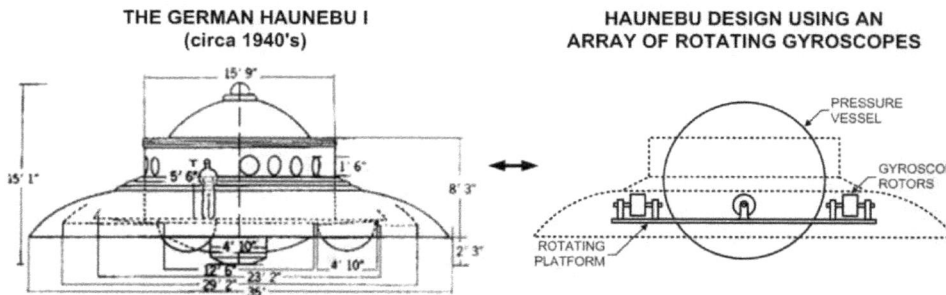

THE GERMAN HAUNEBU I
(circa 1940's)

HAUNEBU DESIGN USING AN
ARRAY OF ROTATING GYROSCOPES

Photos of the Channeled Script of Maria Ortisch

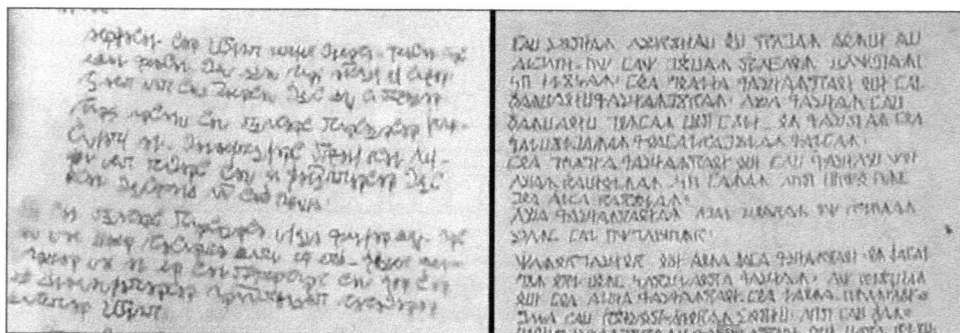

Templar Known German Script

Ancient Sumarian

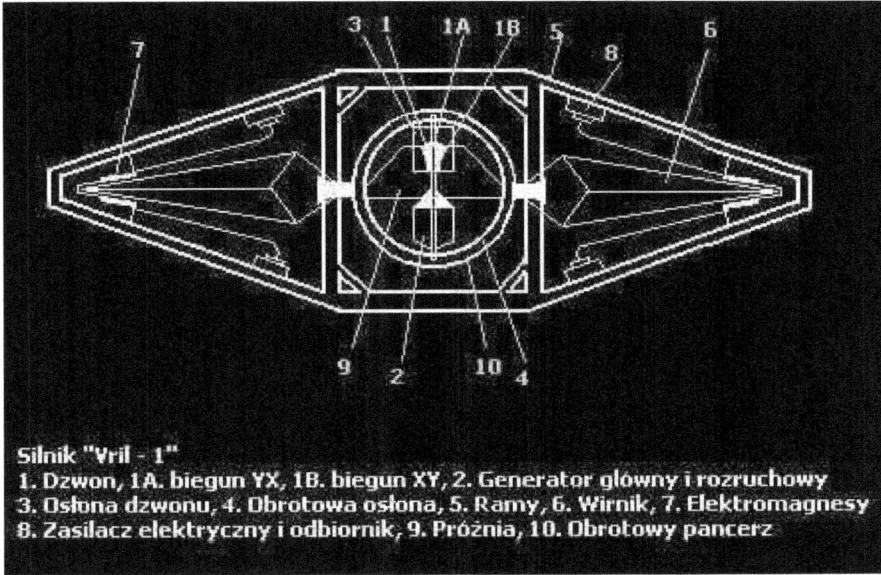

Silnik "Vril - 1"
1. Dzwon, 1A. biegun YX, 1B. biegun XY, 2. Generator główny i rozruchowy
3. Osłona dzwonu, 4. Obrotowa osłona, 5. Ramy, 6. Wirnik, 7. Elektromagnesy
8. Zasilacz elektryczny i odbiornik, 9. Próżnia, 10. Obrotowy pancerz

Sketches and illustrations of the Vril Craft

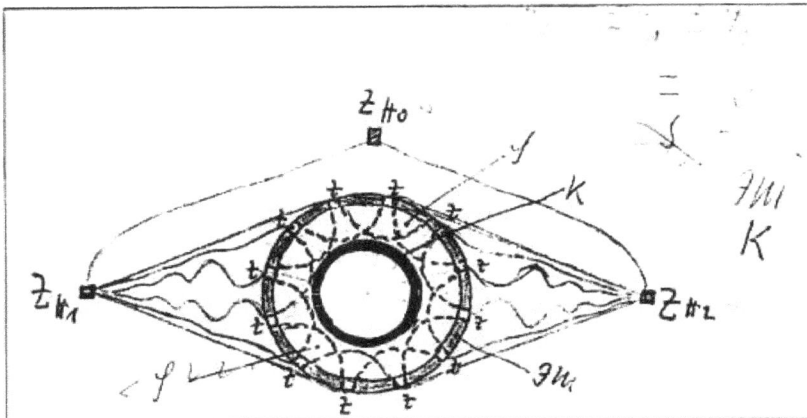

Abb. 3: Schumann-Trinks-Entwurf von 1944. Bundesarchiv Militärarchiv Freiburg, Nachlaß Schumann

Overall dimensions of the bi-conical Plasma Pinch Atomic warhead developed by Schumann & Trinks 1942-1944 with a 5kg Uranium 233 sphere

Z = symbol for plasma pinch

20 cm (8 inches)

3.93 cm

20 *Rainer Karlsch*

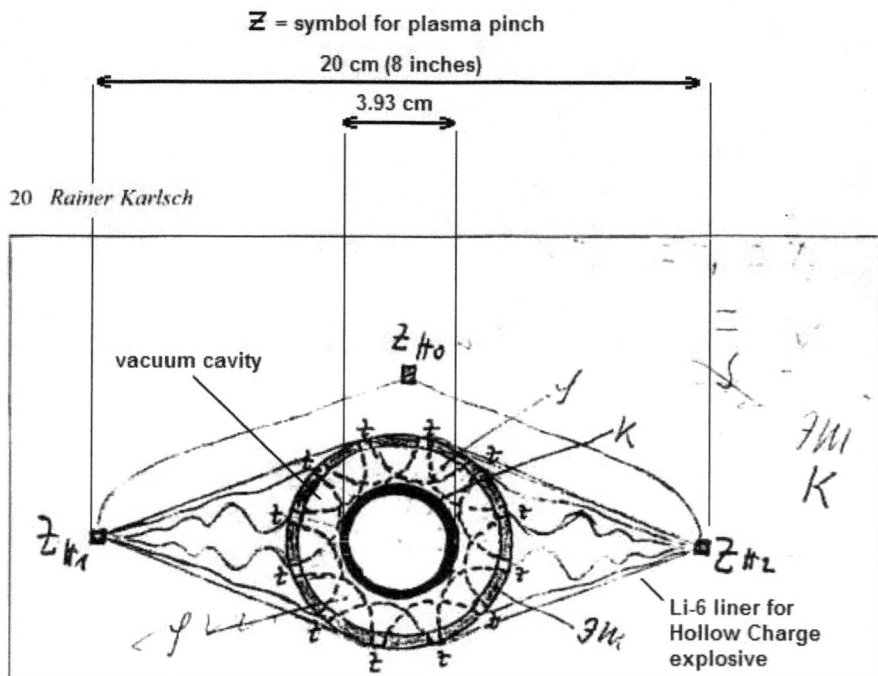

vacuum cavity

Z H_0

y

K

Z H_1

Z H_2

K

Li-6 liner for Hollow Charge explosive

Abb. 3: Schumann-Trinks-Entwurf von 1944, Bundesarchiv Militärarchiv Freiburg, Nachlaß Schumann

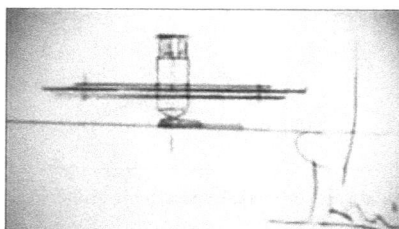

Advanced Designs

Vril 7   Schnittbild mit Antrieb   Mannschaft

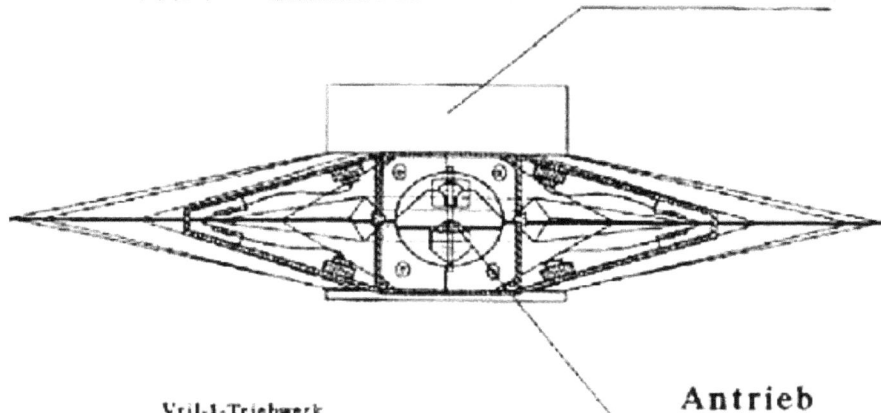

Vril-1-Triebwerk   Antrieb

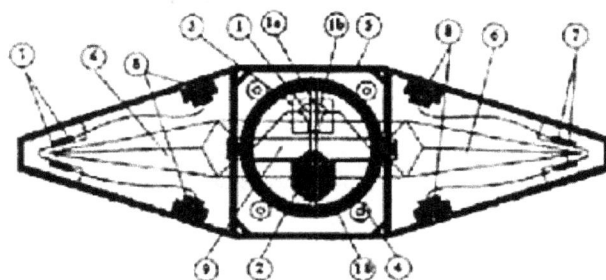

1	Glocke	4	Schwingungseinschluß	10 Schwingungsspeicher
1a	YX - Pol	5	Rahmen	
1b	XY - Pol	6	Drehkörper	
2	Haupt- u. Anlaß	7	Elektromagnete	
	Generator	8	Stromspeiser u. Aufnehmer	
3	Glockenmantel	9	Vakuum	

Gemeinschaft des Schwarzen Steins

Rekonstruktionsversuch   **Durchmesser des Geräts ca. 45 m**

This is a photograph of a Vril Designed Craft made by Germany. In the above photo you can get a grasp of the dimensions of this Vril Design Craft by comparing its size in regard to the tank, truck and people in the photo.

Dr. Hans Kammler. Responsible for Haunebu development late in the war.

Chapter 1: The German Haunebu Designs

Dr. Hans Kammler.

Dr. Hans Kammler's Haunebu Designs

Vermutlich Schauberger-Gerät mit Winter-Tarnanstrich
(Raum Augsburg 1939)

HAUNEBU I

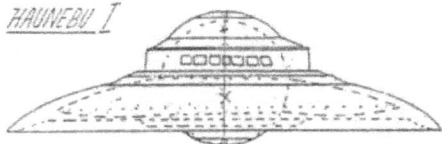

1939, 25m diameter

HAUNEBU II

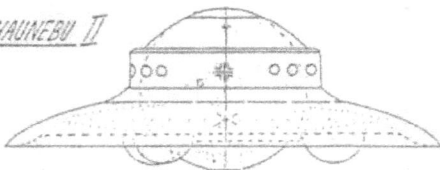

1942, 26m diameter

HAUNEBU III

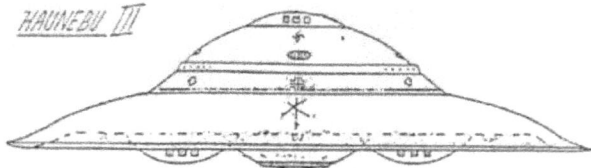

1945, 71m diameter

HAUNEBU IV

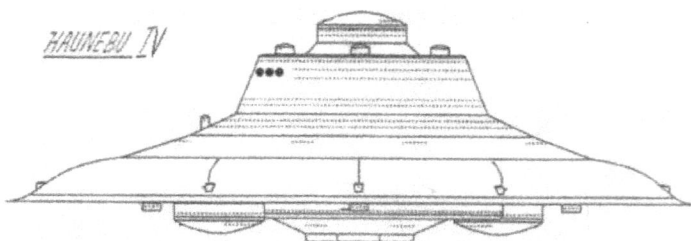

1946 (planned), 120m diameter

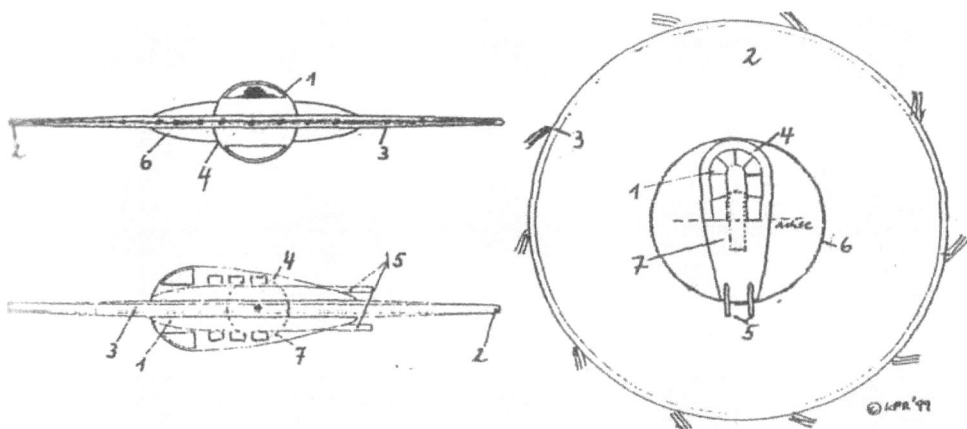

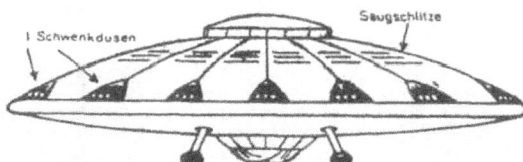

Ballenzo – Schriever – Miethe – Diskus
Start- und Landebeine,unten aufblasbare
Gummipuffer, ein- und ausfahrbar
Ingenieurszeichnungen

HAUNEBU III

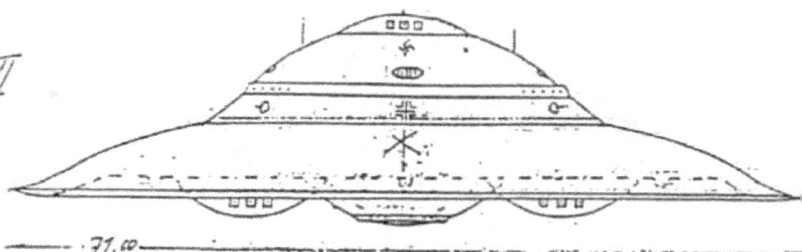

71,00

SCHWERER BEWAFFNETER FLUGKREISEL „HAUNEBU III"

Durchmesser: 71 Meter
Antrieb: Thule-Tachionator 7c plus Schumann-Levitatoren (gepanzert)
Steuerung: Mag-Feld-Impulser 4a.
Geschwindigkeit: ca. 7000 Kilom. p.Stunde (rechnerisch bis zu 40000)
Reichweite (in Flugdauer): ca. 8 Wochen (bei S-L-Flug 40% mehr)
Bewaffnung: 4 x 11cm KSK in Drehtürmen (3 unten, 1 oben), 10 x 8cm KSK
in Drehringen plus 6 x MK 108, 8 x 3cm KSK ferngesteuert
Außenpanzerung: Dreischott-Viktalen
Besatzung: 32 Mann (erg. Transportverm. max. 70 Personen)
Weltallflugkeit: 100 %.
Stillschwebefähigkeit: 25 Minuten.
Allgemeines Flugvermögen: Wetterunabhängig Tag und Nacht
Grundsätzliche Einsatztauglichkeit: Etwa 1945.

Bemerkung: SS-E-IV hält den Hinweis für notwendig, daß in
„Haunebu III" ein großartiges Werk deutscher Technik im ent-
stehen ist, wegen der allgemeinen Materiallage aber alle
Kräfte auf das schneller verfügbare Haunebu II gesetzt
werden sollten.
Gemeinsam mit dem leichten Flugkreisel „Vril" der Schumann-
Gruppe könnte „Haunebu II" die vom Führer aufgestellten
Forderungen sicherlich erfüllen.

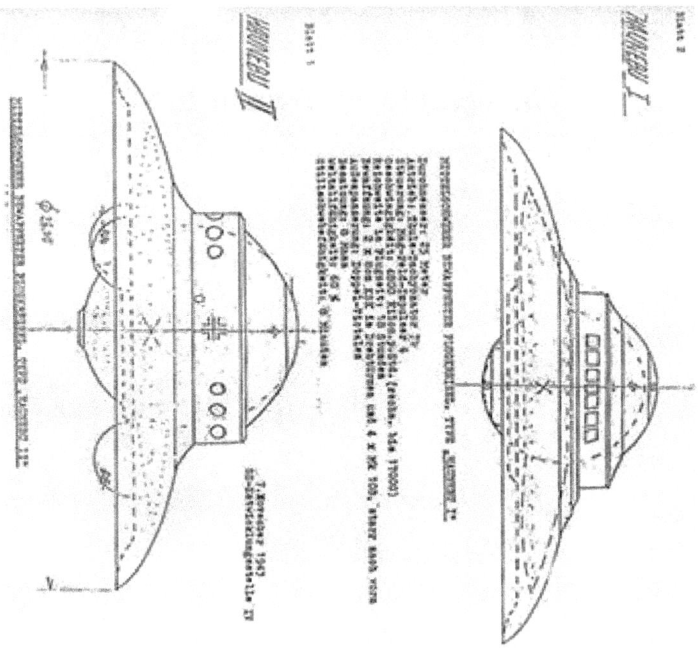

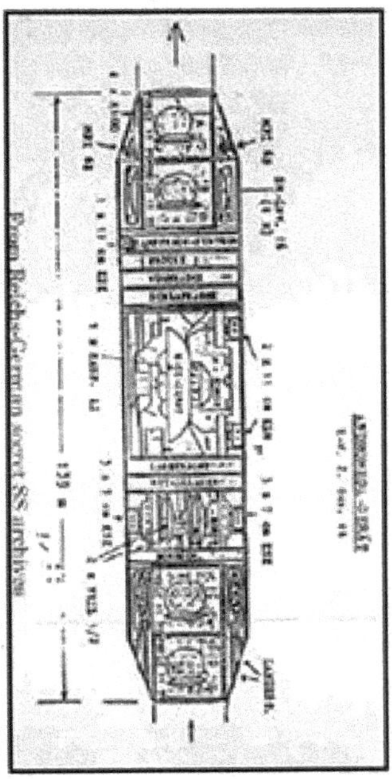
From Reichs-German secret SS archives

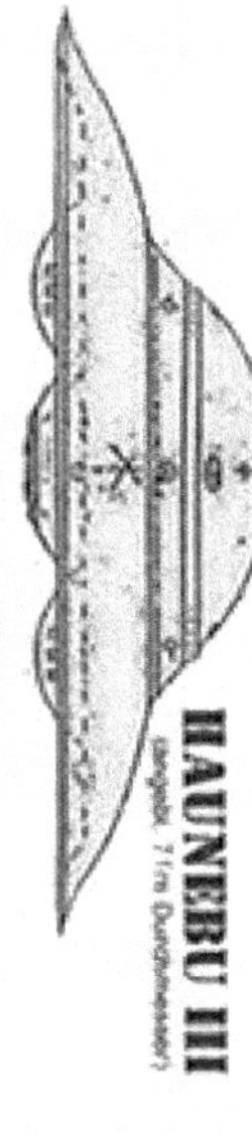
HAUNEBU III

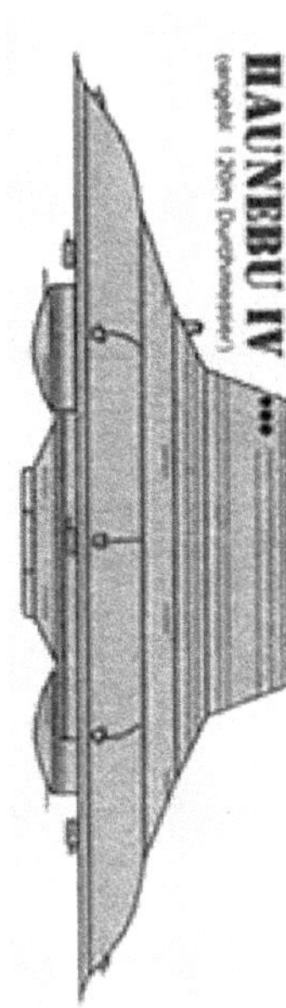
HAUNEBU IV

Photographs of German UFOs

Wewelsburg is a Renaissance castle located in the village of Wewelsburg, which is a district of the town of Büren, Westphalia, in the Landkreis of Paderborn in the northeast of North Rhine-Westphalia, Germany. The castle was completed in 1609. It has a triangular layout - three round towers connected by massive walls. After 1934, it was used by the SS under Heinrich Himmler and was to be expanded into the central SS-cult-site. After 1941, plans were developed to enlarge it to be the so-called "Center of the World". In 1950, the castle was reopened as a museum and youth hostel.

Designs for Wewelsburg Castle

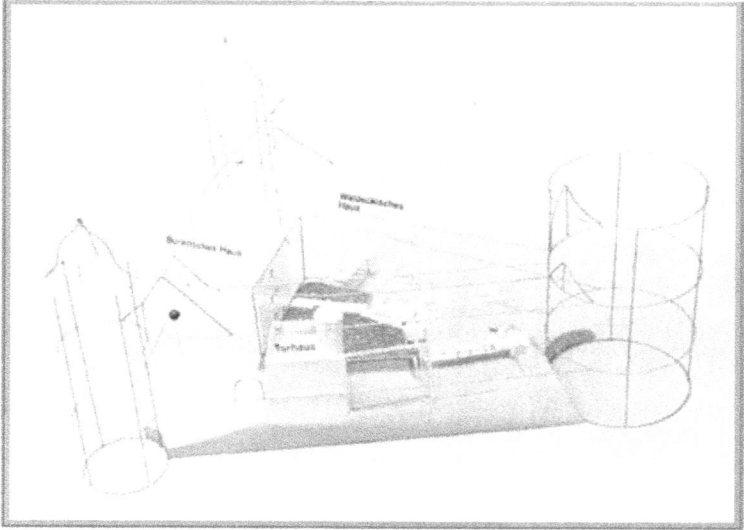

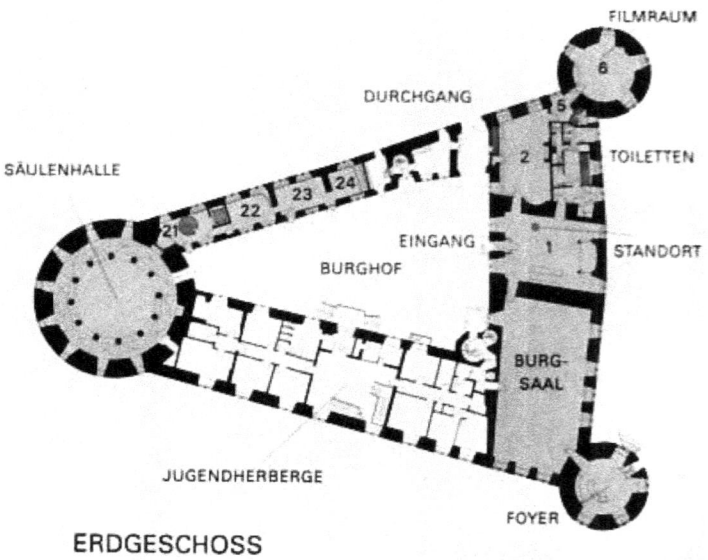

ERDGESCHOSS

The Black Sun

The term Black Sun (German Schwarze Sonne), also referred to as the Sonnenrad (German for "Sun Wheel"), is a symbol of Vril energy used by Aldebaran ships and Chime. Its logo is based on a sun wheel mosaic incorporated into a floor of Wewelsburg Castle during the Nazi era. Today, it may also be used in occult currents of Germanic Neopaganism, and in Irminenschaft or Armanenschaft-inspired esotericism, but not necessarily in a racial or neo-Nazi context. Despite its contemporary use, the Black Sun had not been identified with the ornament in Wewelsburg before

1991, although it had been discussed as an esoteric concept in neo-Nazi circles since the 1930s.

The Swastika an Ancient Symbol

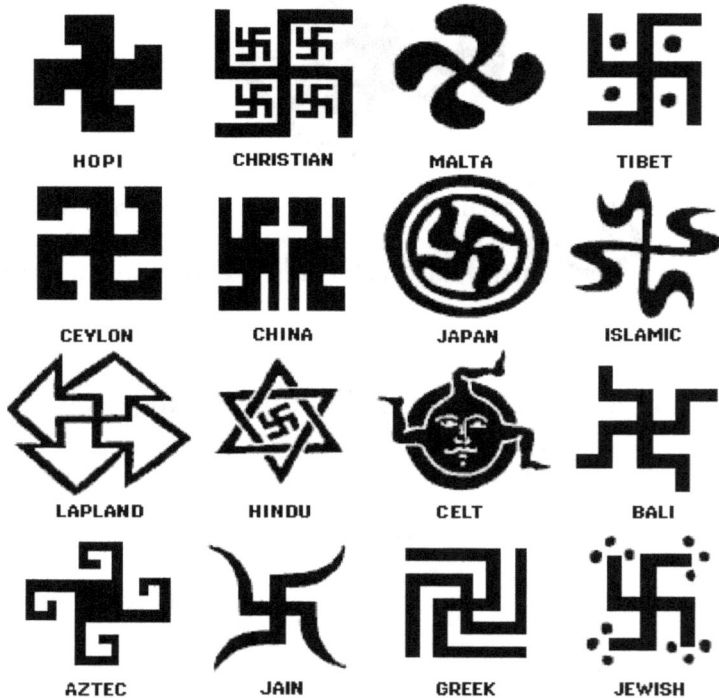

HOPI	CHRISTIAN	MALTA	TIBET
CEYLON	CHINA	JAPAN	ISLAMIC
LAPLAND	HINDU	CELT	BALI
AZTEC	JAIN	GREEK	JEWISH

The Swatstika best known by the use of the Nazi Party is actually an ancient symbol used by cultures all over the world. However the negative emotions now attached to it has created a censored and distorted history of this symbol.

The Black Sun Inside Wewelsburg Castle, Germany

Chapter 2:

What Exactly is Human?

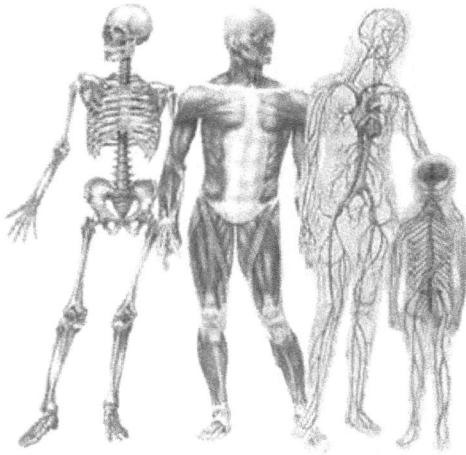

Chapter 2: What Exactly is Human?

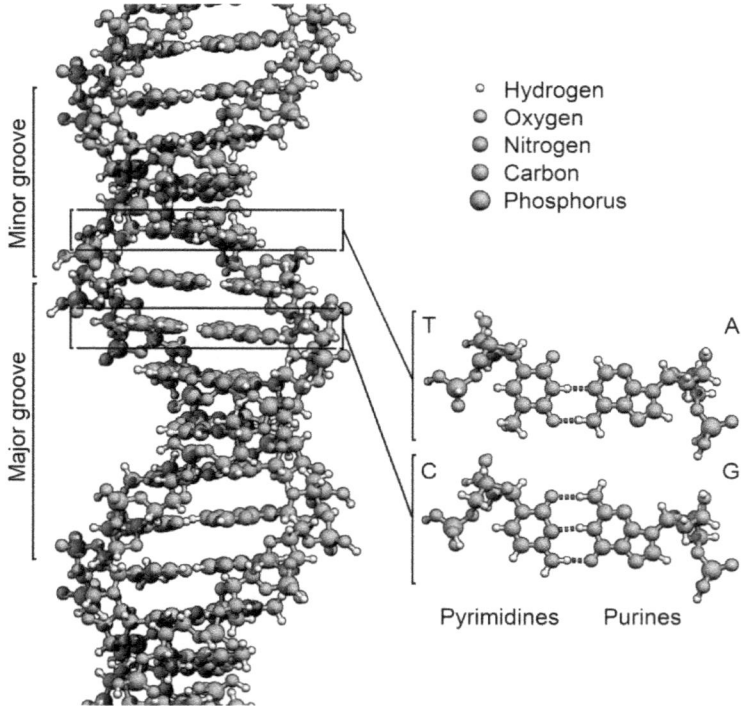

Hydrogen
Oxygen
Nitrogen
Carbon
Phosphorus

Minor groove

Major groove

T   A

C   G

Pyrimidines   Purines

Chapter 2
What Exactly is a Human?

need to cover some background material here before I can get into further details. The basic answer is that a Human is actually a waveform. A very complex waveform is more exact. In order to discuss this I need to provide some basic information on waveforms. This series will use the simplest methodology for expanding an understanding of waves.

THIS IS A BASIC SINE WAVE:

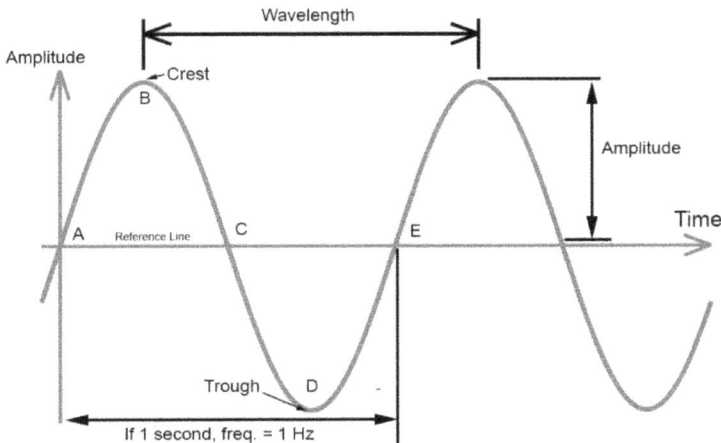

Chapter 2: What Exactly is Human?

Of course the human is much more complex than the previous image can carry, but it is useful for the explanation of the ideas. The wave intersects the neutral point at point A, C, E, and so on. These points are important, for this explanation.

The first concept here is an additive set of waves:

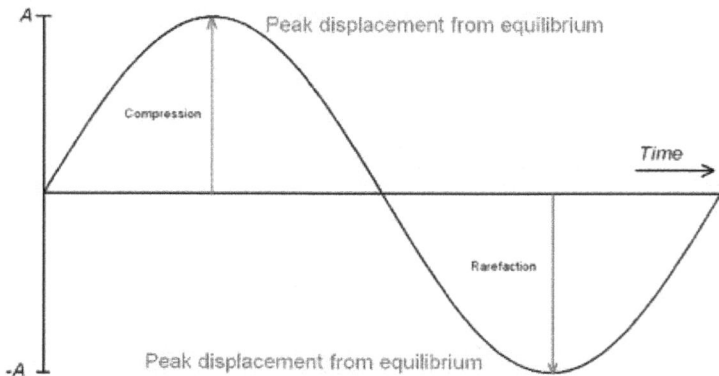

This image shows the wave in a 2 dimensional format with time proceeding from left to right.

Chapter 2
What Exactly is a Human?

If you have Wave 1 :

And then add it to Wave 2:

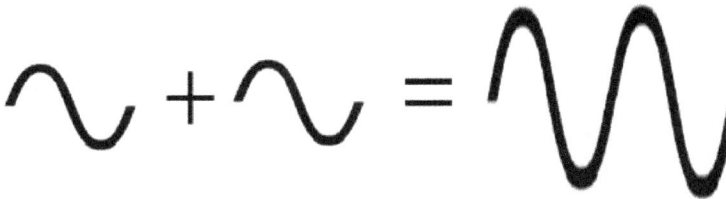

$$\sim + \sim = \wedge\wedge\wedge$$

The result is additive:

This has increased the wave strength, but has not altered the frequency of the wave. In a manner of expression the new wave is more powerful than the original two waves.

Chapter 2: What Exactly is Human?

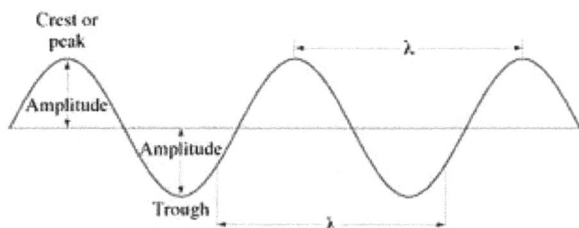

In like manner Wave 1 plus Wave 2 will subtract from each other or cancel each other out:

$$\sim - \sim = \text{———}$$

In this case the new wave has no power in essence it is nonexistent.

Waves may be placed upon other waves making them more complex like these examples:

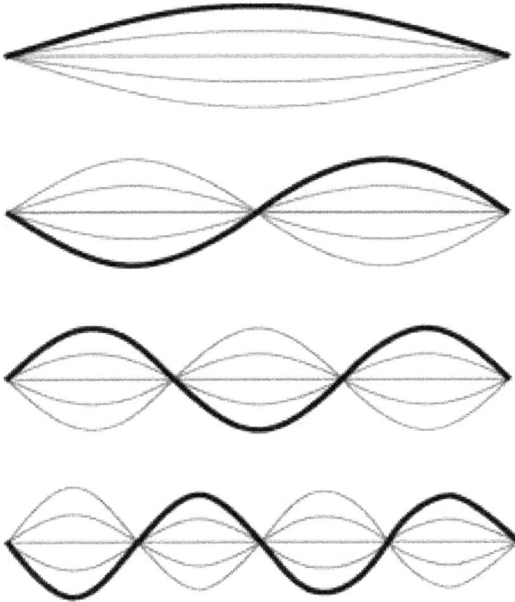

Waves may exist in different orientation to each other

as they are truly 3-D in nature:

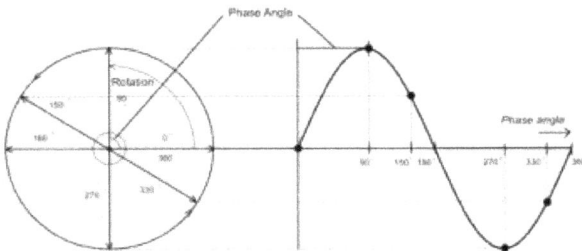

The complexity of a human waveform or even a

simple organism cannot be explained in such a simple

series of diagrams. For a development of understanding we will continue to build upon this.

Each human being has basic wave properties. The magnetic field shown below has a 90 degree phase angle to the electromagnetic wave when viewed from the end.

Propagation of an Electromagnetic Wave

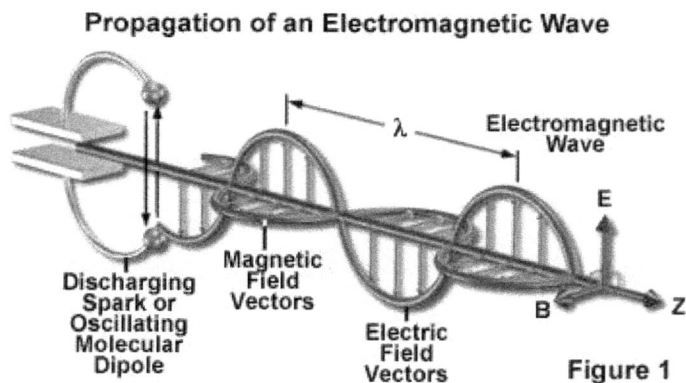

Figure 1

All entities created; what we call Matter, and Anti Matter is a part of all creation called "Mathematic Being." There is another state of being "Chime."

Chapter 2
What Exactly is a Human?

Although this is quite real and important it will not be covered here for continuity of the presentation, and will be explained in another chapter.

Human waveforms certainly have electromagnetic, magnetic, and electrical fields associated with them, and a few other waves discussed later. These waves are not simple sine waves, but since each wave is multiple in complexity it is easy to see how complex this can become.

The human being has millions of waves upon waves, and thus the wide range of complexity in humans is produced. All Human waves have specific sets of characteristics in general. In addition to the waveform, humans can exist in a reality of intersecting light wave patterns called "Matter"; here they manifest as the familiar human body.

One of these complex waves called the "Life-wave" is used as the reference, or vertical wave. This corresponds with the diagram on the previous page; in

Chapter 2: What Exactly is Human?

the up and down, or "E" plane of the diagram. Life in this case means a life in the existence beyond the concepts of space, and time not just a single lifespan on Earth.

Another wave exists in all Humans, which is offset 52 degrees. This is the "Soul-wave", in some instances this may be called the "Mind-wave", and is implicative of free thought, expression, and ideas. Nothing can have any activity at all without the combination of these waves. Everything which exists has these two waves. The phase angles are different for each different creation. Example: A star or a mineral specimen.

The next wave is the "Race Wave", and bares within it a first set of complexities which have produced further uniqueness in humans. This wave is the first big difference in Humans. The very basic methodology of this can be referred to as the dark races, and the light races. The manifestation is skin tone in the physical body. This wave is offset from the "Soul Wave" by anywhere from 6 degrees to 13 degrees, meaning it is from vertical 58 to 65 degrees.

There were two pre-human races before the current Human race, and these have carried forth into the current model. All humans were created from earlier proto human beings combined with another being, or perhaps an "alien" being. These proto humans were barely more than animals in existence so we owe quite a bit to the effort of these "aliens" otherwise we would not exist as we do today.

The "aliens" were not all knowing, and did make mistakes which will be discussed in a later chapter. This genetic program was designed to refine a super power being in order to participate on their behalf in a "Galactic War." However they were defeated before the program they initiated was completed.

Chapter 2: What Exactly is Human?

The "aliens" themselves are a group which split among themselves upon a reasoning of power allocation. They developed many other sub cultures to fight their battles for them.

The subcultures we were modified with came from a planet of mud, and have feet designed for a mud environment. This is why human feet are the least cultured feet of any animal on the planet earth. These "aliens" are somewhat like humans in appearance, and have the same appearance with few if any variations. They are quite mortal, and have little to no ability beyond our own. The "aliens" have been around longer thus acquiring a vast array of knowledge well beyond our comprehension at this time.

Chapter 3:

"The Administrators"

Chapter 3:   "The Administrators"

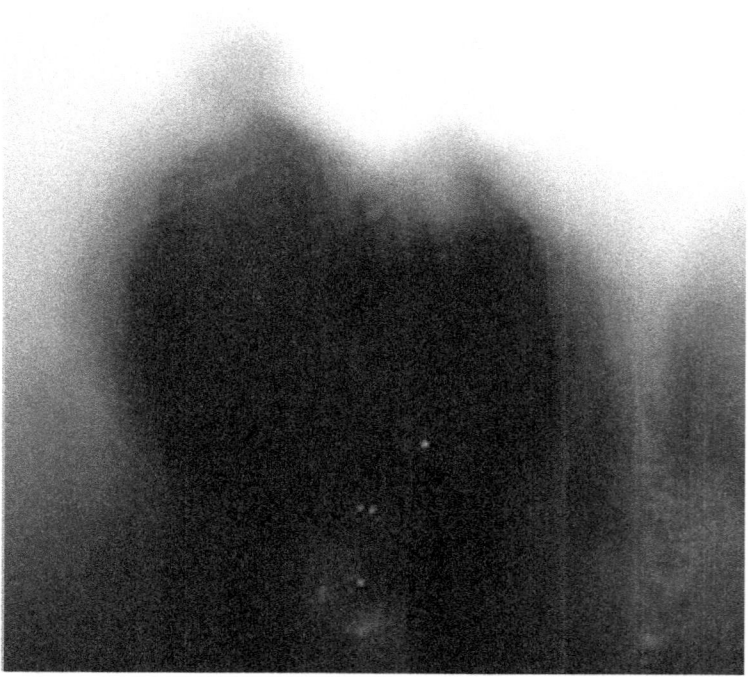

Chapter 3
"The Administrators"

The next event was the arrival of "The Administrators." Who are more or less a neutral party to the Galactic War. This group arrived here to see to it that we did not rise up, and come to the aid of the defeated group of "aliens." The opposing alien side created a counter waveform to the original "alien" waveform, and inserted it into the human Life-wave stream. Due to protest from the first "aliens", they were allowed to create a stream of waveforms also. These streams have a limited number each. These streams were first called the "Dominion," the opposing original aliens, and the "The Children of R" of the originating "aliens".

"The Administrators" more or less treat the affair with a "hands off" approach. If humanity meets certain criteria then they will be allowed to join the universe of beings someday in the future. However if other criteria is reached before humanity meets the

Chapter 3: "The Administrators"

designated criteria of "The Administrators" to join the rest of the Universe; then Humanity will simply be destroyed and thought of as a failed experiment by "The Administrators." The "Administrators" regard humans as horrifically violent, but understand the reason for this as a part of the stated development criteria.

"The Administrator's" Criteria:

§ The denial of hostility.
§ To reach an understanding of the ultimate goal of balancing the universe.

"The Administrators" are of a superior waveform pattern, and cannot be corrupted. This was a part of their creation long before Humans, the Earth, the Solar System and the Universe.

Chapter 3
"The Administrators"

The combined effort of all "Dominion" forces, "Children of R" forces, and the rest of humanity combined are much less powerful than "The Administrators".

Example: An ant compared with a bulldozer.

"The Administrators" could care less if we develop love of all and sharing. The criteria they are looking for is all that is of significance to them. To us this may seem cold, but it is the facts as they stand.

The best way I can describe an "Administrator" for you to be able to comprehend is to compare them to the character "Q" on the television program "Star Trek Enterprise."

"The Administrators" have limitless power like the Race of beings depicted by the character "Q"

Chapter 4:

Aldebaran

Chapter 4:

Aldebaran

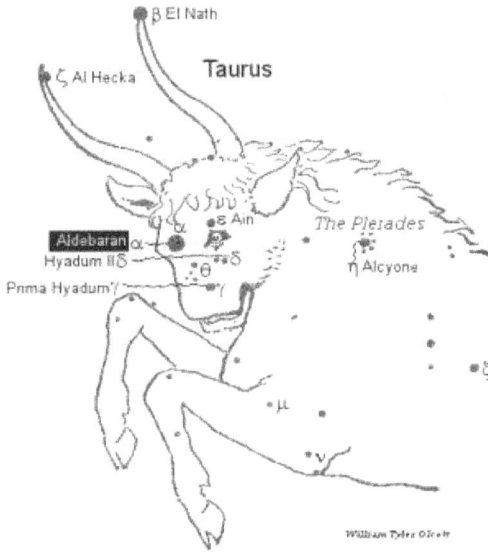

The Alliance of Aliens elected the mild mannered people of Aldebaran, and their higher entities (Chime),which live with them, to represent this cause here on Earth. The Aldebaran's are limited to 33 persons, called "The Aldebaran 33." These were the original "The Children of R on Earth." "The Aldebaran 33" were sent to the light skinned

Chapter 4:

"Aldebaran"

races because of the Life-wave compatibility between these races and the Aldebaran people.

Buddha was one of "The 33 Aldebaran's" sent here originally and has since returned. He has always been "Chime." Many of the stories of Buddha are fabrications and legends. He was one of the "The Children of R" sent here long ago.

Why did the Aldebaran Council decide to stop refilling "The Earth 33" with Aldebaran "Chime?" It was felt that Earth must find its own destiny, good or bad. It was decided by The Aldebaran Council that natives may be better suited to identify with this group.

Each earth native once selected and the title transferred is no longer just an Earth Waveform, but become Aldebaran citizens just like Maria Ortisch.

Chapter 4:

Aldebaran

They are all eligible to become "Chime" themselves someday just as Maria Ortisch. The election of Maria Ortisch to the Aldebaran Council shows the commitment of the Aldebaran citizens to fulfill the role of a true, and faithful mentor to the Earth and its inhabitants.

Not all Earth people will become either Aldebaran citizens or "Chime." The Earth people that are not selected will be able to ascend in a separate evolutionary path. This will only occur if they can throw off the many different influences of the "Dominion."

Why did The Aldebaran's ally with The Reich?

In the beginning of The Reich, and the endpoint of the Weimar, very positive impressions

Chapter 4:

'Aldebaran'

were coming out of that region which would have made the lives of humans easier; a big defeat for the "Dominion." This was reversed by efforts within the large corporations of the Allied Forces, and some corrupt leaders of The Reich. The Reich began to depart from its origins, and became perverse, and many of its leaders became drug addicted. The circumstances were irreversible and The Reich fell into chaos.

Which UFOs are Aldebaran?

There is one large ship which stays very close to the sun. This ship is much larger than the Earth. It was once a warship from the alien wars. The Aldebaran's were reluctant to fight, but had to defend themselves in those days. "Dominion" ships were always cheaply

Chapter 4:

Aldebaran

made so their ship which is also War vintage cannot stay close to the Sun.

The "Dominion" ship is much further out, but it is nearly as large as the Aldebaran ship. Both the Dominion and The Aldebaran's have supply ships docking with these massive old war birds on a regular basis under strict supervision from "The Administrators".

You may note that "The Administrators" which are often found on each of these ships do not have the need for a body. Often "The Administrators" are found in space or on the Earth observing.

The smaller ships from each of these large ships fly to individual planets including Earth on a regular basis. As a general rule: sphere shapes are used commonly by both parties for these tasks. Other shapes include the familiar saucer shapes, tubular

Chapter 4:

'Aldebaran'

shapes, and pyramid shapes are also common. In deeper space there are many other designs including spheres, tubes, pyramids, squares, teardrop, and ring shaped ships are used by both sides. We have placed many of these ships in movies purposefully for you to see the truth. Some saucer, wing and delta shapes are simply Earth (Human) made ships. The Allied Forces confiscated all of the research found and have been constructing ships ever since.

Haunebu type, (Aldebaran Design), made in Germany 1940s, in use by US/NATO until current day, Also reminiscent of an outdated Aldebaran model, all of these older Aldebaran ships are now converted to automatic (self) piloted mode and used for resupply or reconnaissance modes.

Chapter 4:

Aldebaran

Aldebaran Ship Uncloaking

Chapter 5

"The Children of R"

R

Chapter 5

"The Children of R"

The "The Children of R" attempt to send inspiration to humans who allow the creation of various entertainments such as music, movies, plays, literature, and art. In doing this "The Children of R" are providing education against brutal and immoral behavior. All such material has its origin in the "The Children of R".

Chapter 5: "The Children of R"

Who are the "The Children of R"?

"The Children of R" are humans selected prior to birth, born with a Chime and are during their life supplied with a combined knowledge and power. This is of tremendous hindrance to them, but alone they cannot stop the course of events on Earth. All "The Children of R" must educate humanity on what is happening. Please do not wait for the limited number of "The Children of R" to do it. All Humans who have awakened to this must band together, and pass the information along. "The Galactic Councils" are entering a new phase of attempts to constrain the human "Dominion" forces and its allies. Ultimately Earth's fate relies upon negotiations currently being conducted far away from Earth by our group from Aldebaran and is based upon Earth people's merit. Whatever this council decides will be acted upon by "The Administrators."

Chapter 5
"The Children of R"

The "Dominion" know all about these negotiations, and will do anything at all to stop it. Please be aware that nothing to the "Dominion" is sacred, and nothing is beyond their implementation. A general awakening of the human species to all of this information will defeat the "Dominion." The combined Waveforms of humans can brush the "Dominion" aside easier than a breeze can scatter pollen. This pretty much is their only fear.

"The Children of R" Goals:

Their goals are to achieve the Criteria of "The Administrators" for the survival all mankind if possible, to oppose the effort of the "Dominion" forces, to destroy humanity, and to reinforce the human waveforms.

Chapter 5: "The Children of R"

"The Children of R" Methods:

"The Children of R" have a few programs of opposition, and despite being currently less successful in the past several thousand years, a break seems to be appearing.

Section 2:

The programs used by the "The Children of R" :

Mass education of greed and other problems created by the "Dominion"! Even the most neutralized humans seem to recognize that something is wrong although they have neither a way to combat it nor a way to identify it further. This is the product of a device existing not entirely in our realm. It cannot focus full power here, but does have an inspirational effect on the human Waveform. The individuals who have more power of all groups, and races are targeted for the education programs. The method of targeting

Chapter 5

"The Children of R"

has been perfected as of late but strong social norms, the so called racist accusations, and the low ability of resistance of most humans to "Dominion" programs seem to keep this at bay.

The introduction of an Ally; The Ally is a spacefaring community of a common friend of one of our departed "The Children of R". A ship is permanently stationed in orbit around the Sun, and a few bases on some of the planets, and moons to keep watch on the situation on Earth. "The Administrator's" allow this, via tight regulations in order to keep a balance. Currently "Dominion" regular forces outnumber "The Children of R and Earth 33" forces 3 to 1.

A reinforcing wave to aid the "The Children of R" who are hit by the "Dominion" forces weapon. It is not a cure for a "The Children of R," but it is an additive to strength, and does aid in survival.

Chapter 5: "The Children of R"

A camouflage system to prevent more contact with the "Dominion" forces and their wavelength weapon; this is in final testing, soon to be deployed. This will cause false identifications among "Dominion" beings, making them target each other when they think they are targeting "The Children of R."

Exposing of "Dominion" techniques and programs. Examples : False flag events, mass murders cleverly disguised as accidents, or insane persons' attacks on innocent persons. Help from "The Children of R" who have passed, is now being allowed by "The Administrator's" who have seen the extreme evil displayed by the "Dominion".

This is known here as the "The Earth 33 in Aldebaran," a Valhalla for this group. The Waveforms of the departed "Earth 33" are recollected at a location of immense power near the Hall of the Black Sun. Obviously this is a code word for a specific

Chapter 5

"The Children of R"

place. This place contains more beings than just former "Earth 33". Recently this, group was admitted to The Council of All Beings.

Appeals to the Administrator's to get rid of the "Dominion." Negotiations are being conducted. This is why the "Dominion" has tremendously stepped up their campaign. Results will not come quickly, but the Administrators cannot be fooled. Nothing further can be discussed about this. This Book, the goal of this document is to present the facts, known by the "The Children of R" and expose the "Dominion". The "Dominion" is currently recruiting more, and more of the non-committed, and is creating more, and more, less powerful humans (life wave neutralized).

Chapter 5: "The Children of R"

Can I become one of "The Children of R"?

No. First, "The Council at Aldebaran" will more or less choose the appropriate person, and will contact one of "The Children of R" to find the selected person at the appropriate time in their life. This is how the "slots" are filled. All "slots" (33) are full or designated. Persons to fill current open positions are reserved from their beginning before birth for specific persons only no exceptions. To "whom it may concern" money nor influence can get a person a "slot". No amount of money, or fame, or anything else will be able to help with this, sorry. I have to clear the air on this aspect. Actually any amount of celebrity or money truly disqualifies a person, as you must live "below the radar."

Chapter 5

"The Children of R"

Can I join the "The Children of R" in another aspect?

Maybe, if you qualify as a supporter. There are some steps to this process. Those who have something they want to do, may be allowed to be of assistance. Such as distributing books and information, creating mass media to expose the "Dominion" mediumship (channeling), scientists performing investigations, language translating, and other admirable honorable activities are all seen as admissible. Everything is taken before "The Council of Aldebaran" no exceptions. Contact the publisher to forward your information to me if you have such aspirations to join the effort to save Humanity.

Chapter 5:   "The Children of R"

How can you identify one of 'The Children of R'?

The reality is you cannot exactly. You may have suspicions of someone and you may be correct. All of "The Children of R" or "Earth 33" will deny it when asked; this was agreed upon long ago. This may be your best way of telling. All of "The Children of R" live simple lives. They are not rich and are always vigilant of the activity of the "Dominion". Someone saying they are a secret ruler or something similar certainly disqualifies them. "The Children of R" may be the largest group on Earth with the largest amount of posers as their first line of defense.

Chapter 5
"The Children of Я"

Do "Dominion" wavelengths know who "The Children of Я" are?

Yes, but not necessarily who the Earth 33 are.

Are the "The Children of Я" against gun ownership?

No. That is a "Dominion" program, disarmed; the innocent public will be subject to their control, in a faster method.

Chapter 6

The "Dominion"

Chapter 6

The "Dominion"

The "Dominion" is a group of Humans, and aliens who are currently attempting to destroy the opposing group the "Children of R" and Humans. I want to point out the "Dominion" forces are made up of persons committed to a cause and a plan which has been in motion for thousands of years. The "Dominion" want to get complete control of the

Chapter 6:   The "Dominion"

Earth; to slip away from "The Administrators" and ensue in a newly resurrected galactic war by themselves. Ultimate Galactic control is the "Dominion's" intermediate goal then to go forth to other galaxies.

Section 1: The "Dominion's" Goals

There are persons under an extreme illusion which penetrates all the way into their basic Life-wave. The sad truth is that these persons are very well beyond redeemable. "The Dominion" is evil to the core however there are things they are not. To expand on this, they are not all "Grey" aliens (who are "Dominion" allies). They are not fictitious. They are not just general human evil. They are not omnipotent beings. They are not benevolent beings come to help Humanity. They are not all UFO's. They are not groups regarded as evil in the world like Al Qaeda, North Korea, or any warring state. The "Dominion" is more or less a "Branch" of another group who want to

Chapter 6
The "Dominion"

sponsor an end to unity in the galaxy. This does include the "Grey" aliens, shape shifters, and other small bands of remnant alien groups.

The "Dominion's" Goals:

Recruit the Non-Committed to support them without any consideration of facts, or reason. Eliminate "The Children of R" by any means. Eliminate in the end all humans by continuously weakening the human Waveform until all variety of calamities produce the ultimate extinction of the majority of humans in such a way they that the "Dominion" will not appear to be to blame for it.

The "Dominion's" Methods:

The "Dominion" has effective programs for weakening the Human Waveform. The Dominion's main method is to neutralize the 3rd most powerful wave, the Race Wave. The two basic human groups have opposing race waves but about equal life waves. This is shown in the example at the beginning that shows opposing waves of the same basic frequency neutralize each other. Therefore the brainwashing, and forced integration of the light and dark skinned races, and produces a neutralization in the individuals wavelengths who participate, and any offspring they produce.

The offspring of these unions are extremely susceptible to being mentally taken over by the "Dominion" forces and continue the weakening of all mankind. Currently the light skinned groups are being targeted particularly the White Race; which will be followed up in the future with the Oriental lighter skinned races. These are being targeted more because of the Race-wave compatibility with the Aldebaran Race.

Chapter 6

The "Dominion"

They have created a severe program of brainwashing of the above goal. The brainwashing program is convincing the target group that they are guilty of an invented crime called "racism" which up to now has been at least partially successful in the "Dominion's" programs.

The elimination of the "The Children of R Chime", from Earth, via a weapon which inserts a new wavelength into the hybrid Human/Chime's Waveform; unfortunately once it is applied it is permanent to the Human part. The wave is increased via multiple discharges of the wavelength projecting machine, which kills the Human/Chime's human part eventually. It is possible if located to kill one in one dose. This requires a very close range of 30 feet or less with exposure for at least a minute. The wave manifests a brain hemorrhage usually although it can produce heart attacks or strokes, retinal detachments and bursting veins. It can also be applied to any Human.

Another technique of the dominion is the creation of skepticism and obfuscation of the true purpose of the "Dominion." Currently this is in full and severe application! The "Dominion" want to create a system of good guy and bad guy, and have weakened humans identified the "Dominion" with the good guy. Absolutely no real full strength human would believe this, however in the current weakened state of human beings to take this in, as of late.

Sayings like, "you are either with us or against us" is a direct sign of this, as normal conditions would naturally include; a negotiating stance, reasoning stance, a neutral stance, or a leaning (either way) stance.

Chapter 6

The "Dominion"

Create more pollution and more unhealthy conditions to further weaken humanity. This increases every day. When you look at chemical pollutants, genetic pollutants (like GMO foods), electronic radiation from power grids to cell phones, toxic sprays from aircraft, poisons, and lab made diseases spread over the world, drug addictions (legal or illegal), not to mention biological, chemical, and nuclear warfare devices. It is no wonder that humans are less healthy every year.

Create so much disinformation that weakened humans cannot locate the truth. The low approval ratings of government control of the mass media by the "Dominion" and false flag events are all hallmarks of this program. The masses are misled by all variety of made up "facts" that the opposite sometimes seems reasonable. The "Dominion" leadership has an Ally or perhaps better said, a sponsor. This is what we call the

Chapter 6: The "Dominion"

"Grey" aliens. These are beings who support the opposition. To an extent "The Administrators" have allowed them in on a very restricted basis. "Grey" aliens are under specific limitation due to a need for their reproductive system and its ties to earth. Expect multiple problems due to them.

Can I join the "Dominion"?

Maybe, but it depends upon what you can do for them. After they obtain all they can from you please rest assured they will dispose of you in the most expeditious manner. All I can offer here is: "buyer beware!" In any case, I am not the one to contact on this matter.

Do "Dominion" Life Waves know who "The Children of R" Chimes are?

Yes.

Chapter 6

The "Dominion"

How can you identify a "Dominion" person?

This is not so hard. Most "Dominion" human allies are very narcissistic, and usually have money earned via dubious manners. Some inherited it, and when traced back it was obtained from some variety of criminal or immoral method. On the inside these persons are always weak, and insecure, but appear fierce outwardly. Most "Dominions" are homosexual, bisexual, and/or child molesters.

All of the "Dominion" forces are filled with hate, suspicion, ill behavior at times, and are very accusatory. All rich people are not necessarily "Dominion" but the majority of the super-rich and those in seats of power do serve the "Dominion" forces.

All of the "Dominion" forces are deceptive, and their use of "glamour" is very strong. Do not attempt to oppose them yourself. Look for the signs. Keep in mind they must interact with each other from time to time since their true power is weakened. Freaky weird ceremonies are enjoyed, situated, and paid for by the "Dominion". There will be on the fringes of their life, very odd deaths, and disappearances.

What can I do about the Dominion?

You can resist their programs!

Chapter 7

Current Problems Caused by the "Dominion"

It's no secret...

Chapter 7: Current Problems Caused by the "Dominion"

Section 1: Multicultural Programs

Section 2: Drug Programs

Section 3: Pollutants

Section 4: Magnetic and Radio Frequencies

Section 5: Male Feminizing

Section 6: Governments and Influence from Debt

Chapter 7:

Section 1: Multicultural Programs

Currently these programs are specifically targeting the Caucasian countries, specifically the European Union and also the United States. To a slightly lesser degree, other countries like Australia to South Africa are in some state of this stated series of programs. The program basically imports individuals, mostly poor and crime ridden into these countries along with a massive media propaganda campaign to blend with these people. The goal is to neutralize the power base of the people. Sooner or later other countries will be added to the list; Eastern European countries, Israel, Syria, China and Japan to name a few will be targeted by the multicultural programs. In essence Japan will be too Japanese, Israel too Jewish, China too Chinese, and on and on.

Chapter 7: Current Problems Caused by the "Dominion"

Section 2: Drug Programs

Drugs and multicultural issues are "Dominion" caused strife and to an extent have shown some cracks in the system as of late. Multiculturalism has failed even after unbelievable propaganda campaigns. Economies have failed and the host countries have not fallen into this as expected. The EU is in decay and the multiculturalism in the US is also failing, especially as the enslaved underprivileged and poor realize they are being used, to the highest degree. In essence the lowest echelon of society has been re-enslaved under the "Dominion" to do their dirty work, and in the end these people will be destroyed in an even worse manner than the ones they are sent to engage. It is a horrible set of circumstances, and the masses are beginning to see through it. This gives Hope to our cause!

Chapter 7:

Most countries now have all sorts of drug sales mainly pharmaceuticals via illegal and crime ridden sources. This will increase until the citizens cry for legalization then the drugs really begin to deplete the remaining resistance to loss of life power. Basically the removal of incentive is under attack in the drug campaigns.

This seems to be an issue in nearly every country on earth. Some drugs are Doctor prescribed, some synthetic in makeshift and dangerous labs and some are deadly homemade concoctions, and the end is all the same to the "Dominion".

Section 3: Pollutants

The "Dominion" has seen the cracks in the Multiculturalism Programs, and Drug Programs which are currently deployed systems and they have a few more tricks up their sleeves.

Chapter 7: Current Problems Caused by the "Dominion"

Pollution is the newest program. The aerial spray program has almost completely been exposed but the public seems to remain indifferent or unbelieving. A variety of particles and fibers discharged from planes and low level orbiting craft are covering the earth. The fibers seem to have some magnetic capacity and contain dangerous strontium, lead, aluminum, barium and joined with carbon/oxygen fiber matrixes. These fibers have been found in food, water and the air.

Is the Earth Spraying from Aircraft Real? Yes. It is a Dominion program; with 4 or more purposes one is basically to reduce health in the general population. These items to an extent also are added to the air to terra-form the air on earth to a more suitable condition for "Grey's" to live here on a longer basis. This is not to mention spreading toxins and pollutants.

You may know that the Dominion is also spreading this via low level satellites with the ability to

Chapter 7:

dock with larger satellites and reload; these flying labs create the toxins, and refill the spreading satellites.

There are other devices such as trains, trucks, water systems, foods (GMO) and munitions all of which are used from time to time to spread such items. Other purposes are too dumb down the population so it can better be controlled and create all sorts of criminal waves within persons to fed their cause.

Section 4: Magnetic and Radio frequencies

Another is to exercise control of mass populations via magnetic and radio frequencies. Specific radio waves are broadcast to produces a variety of waveforms that change or interfere with normal human life waveforms producing a variety of results. A clear result of this is the severe decline in honeybee population. No part of these programs are in the best interest of the population and do interfere with the life wave forms, causing short lifespans, unhealthy conditions and conduits for dangerous levels of radio and other harmful waves, constantly bombarding the body. The result is increasing cancer, Alzheimer's, and autism on the mild end of the scale, ranging up to disease outbreaks on a interplanetary emergency scale. Animals and plant life are affected as well.

Section 5: Male feminizing

An old trick in the "Dominion's" set of tools is to feminize the male population. In past days this has been used to a higher degree, but in modern times has been making strides. The program has two goals, to increase a less masculine male, which tends to express as a sneaky misfit who undermines everything around him, spreads venereal diseases, increases all sort of criminal activity, integrates well with the multicultural

Chapter 7:

and drug programs, and diverts male decisiveness and leadership to feigning and constant low level pettiness. The feminized male is created via propaganda, prescription drugs, aerial sprays with radio attenuation, and massive propaganda campaigns.

Wars also are planned to eliminate masculinity via combat deaths and injuries. Look for this to increase. It is notable that a counter culture arises which is equally dangerous, this is the over masculinization of the resistant males. This destroys society even further and alienates these males even more than they are already. This also is on the rise.

Section 6: Governments and Influence from Debt

Currently the "Dominion" has several human only groups that the "Dominion" established to do quite a bit of dirty work. These groups DO specifically know who they work for, do not allow them to fool you, they absolutely do! These are investment groups, banking consortiums, oil cartels and drug cartels. Loans are given to governments to influence their decisions, banking consortiums loan fiat money (which is fake money) at huge interests, and flood countries with drugs to influence the government officials. If this does not work they blackmail them with real or 100 percent faked crimes, or just kill them outright. Revolutions, crime waves, mass executions, manufactured diseases, increases in murders and disappearances and many more techniques are employed by "Dominion" controlled human groups.

How can you tell? :

Ask yourself, is the news story on the subject making sense? Are there varied facts which seem to tell different stories or conflict each other? Inconsistencies and outright BS are telltale signs. Most of the big stories of late are just that, "Dominion" controlled

Chapter 7:

fiascos. The "Dominion" is not very thorough and operates very sloppily. Each one is operating at 30%, (maximum) so their own ploy of dividing is working against themselves.

Call them out on the BS they are issuing. When you do so it depletes their power. The more attention brought to their propaganda as false information will raise the doubt level! As the doubt rises, the humans involved, feel less secure and they either run and hide, or "spill the beans" so to speak. Remember an avalanche always starts as a single snowflake.

There is another Dominion movement which promotes "Rights" of almost any social idea. In reality there is no such thing as a "Right", as this indicates "undeserved but granted". In actuality, what is the Truth is "Individual Responsibility".

Chapter 8

How are the "Children of R" & the "Dominion" set up here on Earth?

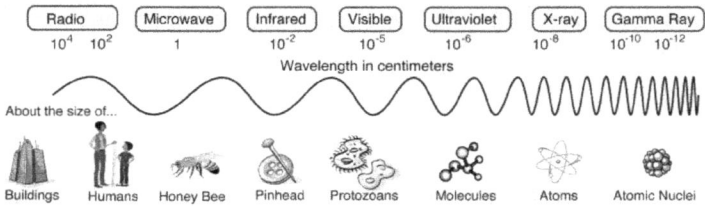

Radio	Microwave	Infrared	Visible	Ultraviolet	X-ray	Gamma Ray
10^4 10^2	1	10^{-2}	10^{-5}	10^{-6}	10^{-8}	10^{-10} 10^{-12}

Wavelength in centimeters

About the size of...

Buildings   Humans   Honey Bee   Pinhead   Protozoans   Molecules   Atoms   Atomic Nuclei

Vril

M

The Children of R and the "Dominion" are here *to convince Earth people to make a decision*, to join one side or the other; which are the previous alien warring groups. Essentially one group is an alliance of many peace loving beings and the other group is an enslaving tyrant race which dominates all it conquers.

how are 'The Children of R' & the 'Dominion' set up here on Earth?

The Alliance of Aliens elected the mild mannered people of Aldebaran and their higher entities which lived with them to represent this cause here on earth, called "The Children of R". The dominating aliens sent some of their minions to represent their side, becoming the Dominion.

"The Children of R" have a limited number on Earth at one time, which are 33. All of these must come from the "heritage of the contacted race" meaning Caucasian, Mongolian or Japanese races. This has to do with the race wave and is not in any way connected to "hate". The "Dominion" came up with a "trick" which is, they split all their positions into 3, giving them a total of 99 positions, "The Administrators", since have made any more "tricks" impossible. However this was allowed since the power of each position was divided to 30% each. The result was that the "Dominion" lost 9% of power in this as punishment.

Chapter 8
How are the 'Children of R' & the 'Dominion' set up here on Earth?

"The Aldebaran 33" was sent to the light skinned races, which has to do with the Lifewave compatibility. All of the 33 were, until recently, a higher entity from Aldebaran called "Chime". In recent times, The Aldebaran Council decided to stop replacing "Chime" on Earth and moved to a program of selecting human souls to fulfill this role, and made these souls Aldebaran citizens.

Previously "Chime" were sent in 3s called a "Chime Triad" along a family lineage. Then the triad system for human soul "The Children of R", was abandoned as well, as this has to do with "Chime" existence not human souls. The family lineage was abandoned as well, but the light skinned race lineage had to be maintained, because of the race wave compatibility with Aldebaran Chime.

Chapter 8
How are the "Children of Ŕ" & the "Dominion" set up here on Earth?

My triad, which was the last sent, born one female born slightly before me then myself (a male), and another female born after me. We were incorporated here on Earth born in various places, and occupy each a sub race of the light skinned race. There are 2 female chimes to one male, this is required to reproduce "Chime" lifespan.

Each of us was identified by the "Dominion" many years ago, and we were incorporated into a military program in a remote wing of the US Government. The "Dominion" thought this would render this triad useless but instead increased the influence of it. The "Dominion" wanted to get rid of the Triad but the US Government wanted to keep it and use it. The Triad rose in strength and the officials recognized that control could not be maintained. Therefore the US Government worked with the

Chapter 8
How are the 'Children of R' & the 'Dominion' set up here on Earth?

"Dominion" to import a weapon to kill the 3 "Chimes".

"Chimes" waveforms are well beyond being able to be fully killed by humans. So they concentrated on a weapon to kill the body of the "Chime". This implies a "reaction time" to replace the "Chime" on Earth; the Aldebaran's responded with a new program for filling the 33 slots.

Chapter 8

Due to the "Dominion's" weapon developed to kill the human component of my "Chime Triad", the 2 females have passed and are not far away, awaiting me. They cannot interact with humans in a direct manner, anymore, unless the human is one of "Earth 33". Currently there are 31 selected humans, and myself which now compromise the "The Children of R/Earth 33." There is one vacancy, which awaits the pre-selected individual, to whom this seat belongs. Each human soul which becomes one of "Earth 33" is assigned a "Chime Triad", and they will always remain in a form of contact with their individual Triad whether in a body, or incorporeal form. The "Dominion" has the same restriction in place. This was designed by "The Administrators" to create a balance, so each place, could choose which direction it would go. The "Dominion" right away decided to split into 3s and ended up with 99, total. The

Chapter 8
How are the "Children of R" & the "Dominion" set up here on Earth?

Administrators quickly moved in and put even more restrictions on the "Dominion", which limits each one's individual power to 30%.; this leaves a total of 9%, this was taken away by the administrators. To sum it up the "Dominion" only has a total amount of power on earth of 91%, compared to the 100% of "The Children of R's". All "Dominion" entities are from other worlds, and exist in a human body for a lifetime.

"The Children of R", attempt to send inspirations to humans, which allows the creation of various entertainment, like music, movies, plays, literature, and art all are providing education against brutal and immoral behavior. All such material has its origin in "The Children of R". The Dominions create control mechanisms, like unfair monetary systems, slavery, inspire all variety of crimes, drug abuse and more to counter "The Children of R's" programs of instruction.

The "Dominion" also attempts to counter the effects of "The Children of R's" information, to redirect, change the perceived meanings, and corrupt the information and so on. Humans actually do the dirty work for them, as actual "Dominion" members never directly seen. These humans are under many influences like greed for money, power, narcissism, and various types of perversions.

Never underestimate the lure of the "Dominion" to get humans to do the most inhumane tasks for them.

In the end the "Dominion" always throws away the native beings like an old apple peel. No human gets to come to their homelands, no human is of any importance to them after they are used. Please know that any "Dominion" promises are completely worthless. Unfortunately, the fate of the planet will be decided on the <u>basis of the majority</u>, and a <u>time limit has been imposed from the start</u>. Please note, that if the decision had to be made today, all Aldebaran Children of R/Earth 33 would be retracted to Aldebaran, and all life on Earth would be destroyed, becoming another rocky asteroid in space.

Steps need to be taken, and this is why the council decided to make this book as a direct method of straight facts. These facts unencumbered by previous programs abilities, such as not paid attention to, over scored by presentation methods or "Dominion" obscuration. Aldebaran's are a mild people and communicate in ways less direct than humans require in these days. We apologize for this simple fact, but we must stress the time is now for all Humans to awaken and rise to the occasion.

There is no hierarchy for the "The Children of R", all are equals and all have contact with the council at all times. "The Children of R" are governed by the Council on Aldebaran. On Earth, all "Aldebaran Children of R Chime" do personally know and interact with "The Earth 33" and sometimes other human supporters. They may interact in many ways, for education or instruction.

Homosexuality, sacrifice and any sort of ruinous ritual is not a part of "The Children of R" operations in any way. Hate is not maintained or allowed in any form, even toward the "Dominion". The "Dominion" have only 33 (of the total 99) who are in contact with their superiors, and are divided into multiple hierarchies, constantly changing as they each vie for power. Due to their reduced power they feel the need to collect together occasionally to make the "feeling" of their power present with them even though they all know it is fake, as they cannot increase in power and they truly have limits in their co-operation due to internal narcissism and hate. These meetings are always bizarre, and appear evil in nature, and almost always include a human sacrifice (usually children), and homosexual rituals at some point. To find out more about all this, look into Moloch. I do not desire to discuss the "Dominion" further.

Chapter 9 :
What Individual Humans Can Do at this Point in Time?

Be stronger than the Dominion...

Chapter 9 : What Individual Humans Can Do at this Point in Time?

Section 1: Resisting Dominion Control

Make no mistake people the Dominion is currently in control, via their human control system. This consists of direct Dominion controllers who oversee humans who work for them directly. Other humans further down the chain only see other human controllers and may not be fully aware of "Dominion" control. All of the humans are fed by just a few techniques used by "Dominion" forces; not only on Earth but in other worlds as well. These techniques are sexual perversions, riches, narcissism, and the power of being in control of other humans. Please know that in the end when total Dominion takeover (under current circumstances will absolutely occur) by the "Dominion", these people will be among the first to be destroyed. In the current day the human controllers will continue to take actions which are horrific, and unbelievably cruel that will be increasing in intensity as time passes. Many people will not like the steps that need to be taken to defeat the "Dominion" due to huge propaganda and brainwashing techniques employed by the "Dominion". It is not too late to fix humanity but the steps must be taken as there is not much time left!

"Dominion" leaders have several techniques developed to achieve control. I have listed these previously but more needs to be covered to allow humans to find avenues to resist. The "The Children of R" have sent actual "Chime" to Earth to aid with this and have selected other humans who have risen in energy of their life-wave to assist. This is a huge endeavor for Aldebaran, and has a huge cost in life-waves upon that tiny community.

Chapter 9 : What Individual Humans Can Do at this Point in Time!

Here is a General List of "Dominion" Imposed Theology Placed in the Human Community:

Firstly, is a notion that all Humans are equal, as any schoolchild knows this is just simply not true, some people are larger, taller, shorter, smarter, fatter, skinnier, less intelligent, and the list goes on and on.

The "Dominion" fights this by a Theological statement that to oppose these facts is in some way a hate crime. Nothing could be further from the Truth! Remember no matter what simple facts are facts, and the statement that "Truth will remain even after the world falls" is absolutely fact. I will say that hate has no place in the Galaxy, but facts are not hate. Another version of this is the Multicultural doctrine, or otherwise known as Diversity. This is a huge deception closely held and widely distributed propaganda from the "Dominion". You must understand that the human races were created for specific purposes. There were several created which no longer survive, because they depleted their life-waves, long ago when they fell for "Dominion" techniques to destroy their race.

Section 2: Rid Yourself of "Dominion" Theology

Today there are 4 major races left. These are Caucasian/Northern Oriental/Aryan; Negroid; Southern Oriental/ Trans Pacific Natives/ American Natives, and Arab. All of these have sub groups. Many people are surprised to see these demarcations. The separations are all within life-wave formats and cannot be described in other ways. Additionally, there are 2 remnant Races left, which are almost wiped out. One is most notably the Basque the other is the Neanderthal. Sexual encounters are, superior methods for transfer of wavelengths. In this way, the

"Dominion" developed a method of convincing individuals it is a good idea to interbreed or at least have sexual encounters between races, to destroy their waveforms. At one point "The Administrators" believed all was lost for humanity due to this false doctrine. Although through significant effort from The Aldebaran Council humanity was allowed to proceed further, as some correction was occurring. Since this time, the correction has been stopped and further "Dominion" propaganda has reversed the tide.

A significant question is, if an individual has participated in this activity, what can be done? Several steps must be taken, and without doubt the main one is to stop this activity at once, and never repeat it. Such an individual is in real and tremendous danger! Their life-wave is severely damaged. Individuals succumbing to the "Dominion" propaganda and who act upon it are tremendously weakened and truthfully could never recover fully from it. The good news is that some energy will be transmitted via Chime, for those who do attempt correction, however full restoration is not an option.

Those who do not attempt correction will pass into the next realm and not have enough energy to exist there in an energy only environment. I can explain this with this example: two individuals of different races had a sexual encounter, and both had a life-wave of 100% prior to this encounter. After this they now have 8% for the follower and 2% for the originator or the idea. The 2% person admitted the mistake stopped the activity, and advised others not to do the same. The individual began relentlessly campaigning against the "Dominion", and was able to build up to 25% before the individual passed to the next realm, but did accomplish many victories against the "Dominion".

This individual will survive as an entity in the next realm, with low energy and after extreme hard work will continue forward, with Chime help. The 8% person continued to have such encounters, and eventually collapsed into debt, sorrow, and wound up addicted to drugs then passed with below 1/1000th of Life-wave energy. The individual does not have enough energy to maintain existence in the next realm and will be dissolved and forgotten. The remaining energy is consumed by Dominion.

Section 3: Essentially this is a last warning for humanity.

Those at or below the 20% range will probably not be able to exist in the energy realm, and face a very serious situation. No aid can be given to those individuals who pass over in such conditions. Appeals to Chime must occur and be granted prior to death. This is the basis of the judgment found in most Earth religions. All negative influences in a human lifespan influence the Life-wave, and those negative activities can lower the energy as well, which will be discussed as well. It is important to reveal this previously held secret, at this time. All lost energy, and the energy from dissolved humans as they pass into the next realm with too low energy in their Life-wave are all gathered by the "Dominion". This is a part of an illegal treaty with the withdrawal of the originating "aliens" who created several of the races. The Council of Aldebaran opposes this but "The Administrators" allow it because it preceded "The Administrators" involvement. Individuals passing in such conditions do not survive as an entity but their energy is eaten in a way of describing the process by the "Dominion". The "Dominion" gets to eat the energy from the Life-wave of individuals involved in prohibited activities. (The "Dominion" cannot do anything to the energy of the Life-wave of the, "Aldebaran "Children of R", Chime(s), and Earth 33. as these are subject to rules of The Council of Aldebaran.) If this applies to you, please know that steps should be taken beyond the ceasing of the activity. Of course, it needs to be emphasized that stopping the activity is a must! The next step is to become a hard worker with the remaining Life-wave energy the individual has, at this point. The denouncing of the "Dominion's" propaganda is the specific activity for such an individual to undertake, (this will attract Chime support). An awakened person in this category has little to lose and everything to gain by opposing the "Dominion".

Another significant question is what becomes of children produced by such a union? Basically it is the same thing as the parents, with one exception. They have little or no Life-wave energy to begin with and they do not belong anywhere. These people are easily controlled by "Dominion" propaganda and the devices made to control such individuals. They should muster all they can to oppose the "Dominion's" propaganda, being as vocal as possible! Such individuals who are children of such unions should not have sexual encounters with any person of a race, essentially staying with other interbreed individuals and produce no children. This may seem harsh; however view this as harshness originating from the "Dominion" toward Humanity, and the control they intend for us. These individuals are straight up "Dominion" victims, and should be effective as a group for opposing them at every opportunity and raising others energy to oppose the "Dominion". Chime will support those who are opposing the Dominion and follow these guidelines. Remember, the "Dominion" is ultimately responsible for this imposed circumstance, and the only avenue to any involvement in interbreeding is total "Dominion" active and blatant opposition!

All Individuals must rid themselves from all varieties of sexual perversions. The main ones in these days are child sexual exploitation, gay and lesbianism. These "lifestyles" are heavily promoted by the "Dominion". All of these activities are brought by several variant methods of transmission. The largest is propaganda, and the second is a bombardment of populations by magnetic waves. The alteration produced by the combined effect is tremendous on specific individuals. The loss of overall energy is shocking and the remaining energy is damage to the specific wave itself. Please if any individual is or has participated in this sort of activity, is advised to obtain spiritual help to reverse this energy, immediately. The consequences are similar to the multiracial encounter.

Unfortunately most will not and face the ultimate destruction. I repeat - For those who can stop this activity, do so, and join in the opposition of the "Dominion." Secondly, rid yourself of all influences Imposed on society by the "Dominion".

Do not fall into the propaganda of Multiculturalism, Drug Abuse, Alcoholism, Male Feminization, Gay/Lesbianism, Usury, Sexual Perversions, Interracial Sex, and Violence. More are employed than those listed but these are the current main effort of the "Dominion". The promotion of one sex over the other is a form of perversion. Anyone with any sense at all knows that women should behave as Women and Men as Men. The sexes should balance and should operate as a team in any venue. Promotion of divorce, domination, and imbalance has been a mainstay of the "Dominion" for centuries. These steps will increase your personal Life-wave, which automatically increases the entire human Life-wave in general. It also helps to ensure the overall survival of Humans to enter into the Galaxy as a meaningful and purposeful unit. Thirdly, oppose the "Dominion" at every opportunity. All humans in a deeper sense are aware of such activity that the "Dominion" engages in. These days the propaganda is thickly applied and the waves transmitted from "Dominion" source machines are great.

The Aldebaran Council is actively protesting such measures and some headway is being made. Even with this activity individuals can resist by

Chapter 9 :
What Individual Humans Can Do at this Point in Time?

communicating truth to others and opposing the propaganda as it comes forward. Some areas are getting very good at opposing the propaganda as of late. Joining in, with the opposition increases the strength of the force against the corruption. Do not allow corruption to exist on any level, from low level supervisors to multimedia news corporations.

Expose any corruption and opposing the "Dominion" influence in business, school, society, mass media and individual encounters will reflect highly for yourself and humanity in general. Act professionally, politely as you possibly can without violence, to make yourself more credible, with your opposition. Fourthly, all Humans must seek advancement. This is essential to reinforcement against "Dominion". The opposition to increasing your own Life-wave, Health, and Esoteric Skills is fierce. The "Dominion" knows they cannot stand against such individuals especially if they unite against them. All people have access to something in all these categories, please learn and practice them against the "Dominion". Each race has a set of esoteric skills which will cooperate with other races efforts, the esoteric skills will combine and could even drive the "Dominion" from the planet if the majority of humans participate. Of course "Dominion" forces have emplaced cultural memes to prevent this which are only false beliefs in reality.

Chapter 10:

Religions

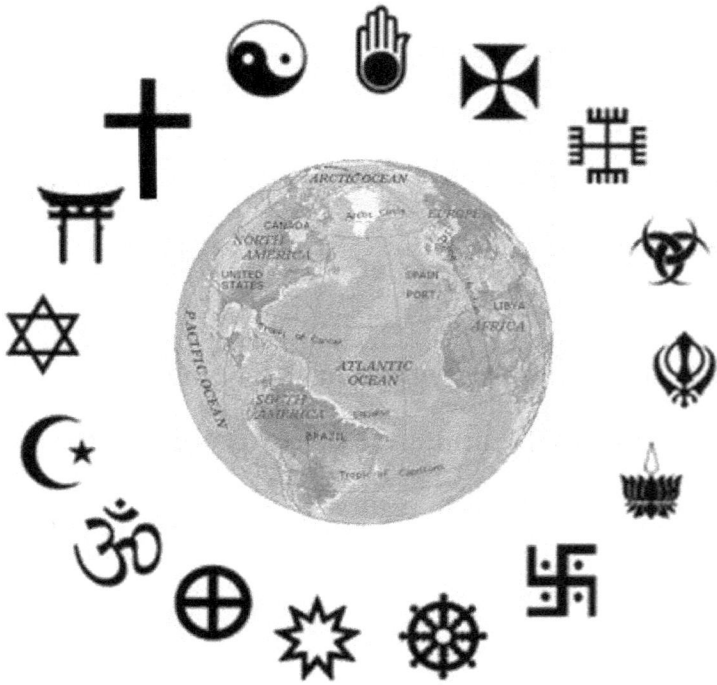

Chapter 10 : Religions

The oldest religion for the area of interest is the correct one for the area, and the people who inhabit it. Using Islam as an example, someone who is of Arab descent is correct to be Islam, or more correctly of a pre Islam religion. Nord/Celtic/Germanic peoples are correct with Wodanist religion, and Native Americans with their tribe's religion. The pattern goes on and on. There was a base religion backing all human wave forms, and religions which are of a more pure lineage, which is Buddhism, and Christianity are a descendant.

Keep in mind that both current day Buddhism and Christianity has been subject to corruption by the "Dominion", and the same is true with all religions. Look for inconsistencies, the presence of homosexuality, child sacrifice, and over regulation of

Chapter 10 : Religions

one's life; and you will locate the places that changes have been made. Maria Ortisch states, on multiple occasions, "each individual is to work within the system in which they are in to do good for the universe."

Are Christianity &/or Buddhism the correct religion for mankind?

No one religion is the correct religion for all of mankind anymore. However these two, were in the beginning the same religion and share major tenets, even today.

Some components were lost, in the abandonment of Celtic groves and Nordic sagas. Hinduism and Buddhism both have a common origin as well as other smaller religions like Bon Po. I usually address Buddhism as it is more common to western readers sort of representative of all of these in a sense.

Chapter 10 : Religions

Additionally, one of my Triad was raised in the human body as a Buddhist. I suppose it is just a way of relation, on my part. In many ways, Buddhism was a sort of an attempt of reconstruction of the older way, behind Brahmanism, Hinduism and Bon Po. You can add several similar Japanese, Korean, and others into this grouping of which all require research. Of the ones specifically listed above, Bon Po is slightly more close to the root, and should bear studying. I must stress that there exists a current thought pattern in the west about Buddhism, and Hinduism. The loopy, hippie, dazed, way of viewing these religions is just as incorrect as the view of the former Dali Llama (who incarnated before the current one) which was dark and sort of spooky.

This includes a wide modern range of people who live today in Europe, and those of European

Chapter 10 : Religions

heritage residing in other parts of the world; Northern China, Mongolia, Iran, Pakistan, Korea, and Japan. Areas in adjoining countries are included of the same peoples. I do not want to list parts, of this country and that. All of these peoples should get together and recreate their root religion to become more successful. Christianity, was a religion taught by a scholar named Jesus or perhaps better said Yeshua. Jesus was taught by Buddhist and Egyptian monks/priests, and was very much aware of Brahmanism, and other religions. His teachings are wise, and were combinations of the core tenants of these. Please refer yourself to the Beatitudes in the Bible. His stories are teaching allegories meant to describe, and transfer wisdom to a variety of people with many different backgrounds. Jesus preached multiple times about the "Kingdom" is within and not without. This concept is a main tenant of all religions in our galaxy. Close attention should be paid to this, by all humans!

Chapter 10 : Religions

I sense that there are so many viewpoints about Christianity that I cannot cover it in the limits imposed by this book. Perhaps I can say, since it was a sort of reconstruction religion in its beginning, and it has much merit. Since the original teachings of Jesus included many other teachings, in a mutually combined way, it can be viewed as, at least partially correct, for all those people, native to all those religions, if reconstructed. It needs more research to find the most original documentation these days, as all other religions do as well, as the "Dominion" infiltrated it as they do all human religions, via humans who are compromised by the "Dominion".

So you may ask, what is the correct religion for the Caucasian/Northern Oriental/Aryan race and I can say at this point there is no one answer. A reconstructed Buddhist, a reconstructed Christian, reconstructed Wodanist and local reconstructed religions are correct especially when combined with Shamanism, for the White Races. Go with what you know is good advice and give time to research of the older ways.

Section 1: The correct root religion for Caucasian/ Northern Oriental/Aryan race:

Jesus, Buddha and Mohammed were real people. Buddha has the best preserved tradition of his life still intact. Still some errors exist in Buddhism. Buddha was one of "The 33 Aldebaran's" sent here, and has since returned. He has always been "Chime". Many of the legends of Buddha are fabrications and legends but he was one of the ones sent here long ago. Jesus was for real and one of the chosen bloodlines for the "Chime" to reoccur. Jesus was chosen to send messages to certain areas; he returned to Aldebaran

Chapter 10 : Religions

and passed to "Chime" energy state. Some of his teachings were modified at later points, by the "Dominion" for control of humans. It is important to note that the real Jesus (Also a Chime) was teaching quite a bit of mysticism from Egypt and wisdom from Buddhist sources, as he was trained in both traditions. There is no doubt in any circle that Jesus was a wise teacher and is worthy of study. Mohammed was a real man of chosen (Chime) bloodline and after his death returned to Aldebaran and passed to "Chime". His life was combined in a literary sense with two other men, (one a criminal) but in minor ways only. It was done by the "Dominion" also for control purposes. The pure information presented by Mohammed is of a pure strain and is correct for the Arab desert peoples. Particularly the Sufi sect has preserved many truths which should be considered as among the wisest on earth. Abraham and Moses are legendary figures built up from previous legends. There is no basis in a real person for either of them. The "Dominion" has influenced these and other now defunct legends for control.

Section 2: Jesus, Buddha, Mohammed, Abraham, and Moses:

In all religions the requirement to spread that particular religion to the world is "Dominion" influenced to cause strife between otherwise peaceful peoples. Everyone should take note of this simple fact. No single religion is for all peoples!

Are any of the teachers above on The Council of Aldebaran?

Chapter 10 : Religions

No. They were before and are now "Chime." Humans technically, do not become "Chime" but can achieve a similar but different, state if earned, called "symbolically" Roh-Nah-N, but here will be referred to as Chime for textual purposes. These teachers now are a part of an advisory council to the Council at Aldebaran, made of both Chime who has since returned to Aldebaran. They advise the council on Earth matters. The Council of Aldebaran frequently cannot identify with the extreme activity of some Earth people, since these Chime lived here on Earth they give insight to life on this harsh planet. Aldebaran's are of a milder Lifewave compared to Earth Lifewave.

Can Earth teachers influence humans from their Roh-Nah-N state?

Yes, but it is limited to information, given in something similar to what humans call visions. The "Dominion" can do this as well, so be careful to vet all incoming information to ensure its true source.

I think God talks to me, is this actually God?

No. It is a non-corporeal being, some work for themselves, some for good and some for evil. Many are hired by the "Dominion" to influence desired peoples. All of them can provide good solid information, (or not) if it is their desire.

I find the term paganism as almost undefinable these days as it tends to refer to anything other than what a particular person's belief system is. For example a Sunni Moslem may view a Buddhist as a pagan or a Christian may view a Shaman as a pagan. When referenced to a form of Earth or Nature, it is basically a form of near pre human belief systems, specifically

Chapter 10 : Religions

before the "aliens" modified humans. This means the pre alien human just observed the local environment and made some basic assumptions about life Nature and death. To some nowadays, it may only refer to Earth environment and not the variety of Lifeforms which are out there. Some Lifeforms in our galaxy are well beyond human comprehension. Paganism from my point of view today seems to include extreme viewpoints which are simply wrong.

In a true sense it is the primitive (pre alien intervention) human religion, and in that sense has purity to it if practiced in that way. I do not include actual religions lumped into this pagan category (like Wicca, which is another religion). I am going to allow myself to appear uncommitted on paganism due to the fact that it is relatively undefinable. If you find it useful to your Life-wave, and you do not incorporate the extremes I have no problem with it.

Chapter 10 : Religions

Shamanism is absolutely the oldest human type of religion. It has many commonalities of religions found all over the galaxy. This means in the larger sense it is the true catholic religion, in the true sense of the word catholic (meaning universal). A main tenant is the "going within" to find truths. This may be expressed in many ways, as a journey, as an animal form or other visualization.

Chapter 10 : Religions

Chapter 10 : Religions

Section 2: Nature Religions & Shamanism

This is actually the root basis of all religions within the galaxy. A variety of this is practiced in much of the Aldebaran religion. Shamanism varies in humans from culture to culture. If you are drawn to a form of Shamanism and want to practice this religion please do so. I can say that Shamanism can be practiced by any human Life-wave with attention to personal research as practiced by specific ancestors as there are still many differences between areas. I was raised as a human child here on earth in a form of Shamanism combined with another religion, and I am glad this was the case for me. All human religions need redefinition and research as they all contained inner wisdom and truth at some point, it is a tragedy to humankind that for personal gains all human religions were easily infiltrated by the "Dominion" in attempts to mislead large groups. Just view a few instances of

Chapter 10 : Religions

the daily news and it is easily observable, of the ongoing destruction caused by "Dominion" intervention in religions. Please note there is another underground style "Dominion" program to promote division and destruction toward specific religions. Here I can provide examples, the Sunni vs Shia Muslims, and Northern Ireland Christians; the list goes on and on. Please use caution and personal research if you are in an area where you may be affected by such "Dominion" supplied conflict.

Chapter 10 : Religions

Section 3: Jews and Judism

Are Jews evil?

By answering the question, I must first expand upon the word Jew; if the question is about the people of Abraham, and/or Moses, the answer is inherently, no. These people today are called Palestinians. Palestinian's conducting various act of evil does make them evil, however opposition of the oppression they are subjected to does not make them evil. The government calling itself Israel, in modern times is actually a "Dominion" created system, to promote influence on various religions and produce evil in all of them. These people are actually from the area near the Caspian Sea, and were once call Kazars. Individually these people are not inherently evil, however support of varieties of perversions, and the "Dominion" controlled government does make them evil, in those

Chapter 10 : Religions

regards. The answer is not so cut and dry. Individuals must make up their mind which side they support, and this will either clear them or propel them into evil. Without any doubt, the intentions of the Jewish Nation are definitely within the Dominion's firm control.

Chapter 10 : Religions

Section 4: Islam

Is Islam bad or evil?

No. Islam (or better said the Pre-Islam faith) is the correct religion for a people living in the area at or around the Arabian Peninsula. All places have a correct religion; this is a problem for many areas as they cannot fulfill their true purpose without their correct religion.

Chapter 11

The Races

This is a big one.

Chapter 11

The Races

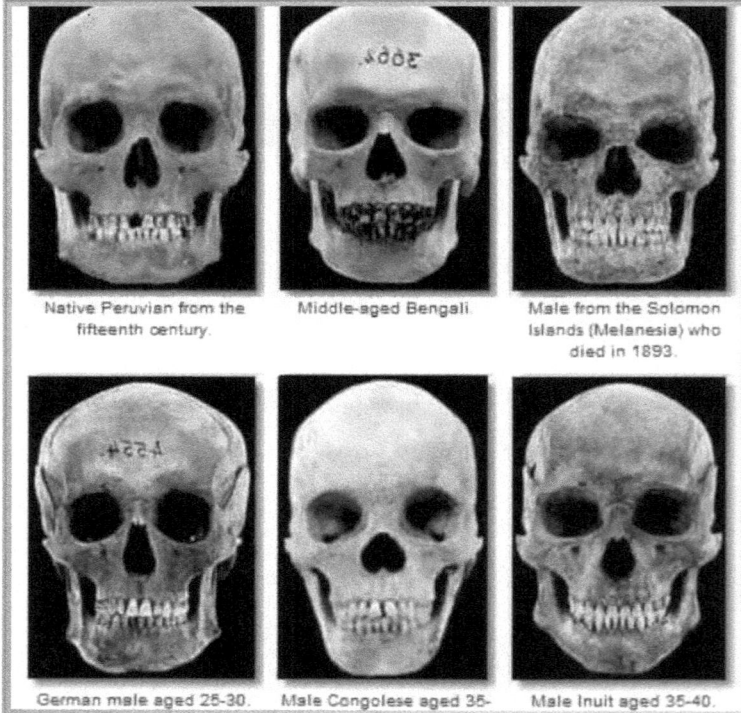

Native Peruvian from the fifteenth century.

Middle-aged Bengali.

Male from the Solomon Islands (Melanesia) who died in 1893.

German male aged 25-30.

Male Congolese aged 35-

Male Inuit aged 35-40.

The purpose of this chapter is to clarify that there truly are distinctions between the human races and each race serves an important purpose, some call this racism, but it is a fact not everyone is created with equal abilities, looks, capabilities, qualities, and etc.

Chapter 11

The Races

To start off I want to directly address the question:

"Are you Racist?"

Absolutely not! Actually I am a supporter of each race! I will do anything I can do to further the redemption of the Human Race and any Individual Race among Humans! A large part of the book is devoted to this material. The human race is falling into multiple traps, designed by "Dominion" leaders to destroy humans from within and this one is very effective at the moment. The "Dominion" thrive on Human destruction and suffering.

All races have a purpose, and each should fulfill its purpose. Each race had a religion in antiquity, and this is a part of the race. Each race should recreate its original religion in order to be complete again.

Chapter 11
The Races

The entire universe is against racial interbreeding and interracial sexual contact which is considered a form of perversion. I concur with this as it destroys an individual's Life-wave, and makes it impossible to exist in the next form of existence, which is an energy only form, even if it is only transitional.

Do you hate Blacks/Negroid race individuals?

No. I will help them to achieve their race's goals as I would any other race. I do not personally hate anyone.

Why are Black races significantly different from the other races?

Chapter 11
The Races

This race was created for entirely different purposes. This race was created on earth for replacing onto another planet, which has a very different climate. The physical bodies of member of this race are very different in certain placement of bone fulcrums and muscle emplacement. The Life-wave is different as this planet has a different wave of its own, from most other planets. Various minerals, on this moist planet, were to be mined and provided to the proto aliens by the Negroid race, in trade for various items and supplies. A war was lost prior to this activity. The planet, which was to be the intended home world for the Negroid race still waits, as the alien forces retreated from it long ago.

To respond to the question, Negroid race individuals have a remarkably different set of harmonics in their Life-wave, and are not compatible

Chapter 11
The Races

with any other race on our planet especially in interbreeding, and sexual activity. In such occurrences both persons are essentially reduced in power. With severely depleted life-forces few people are able to reach stability again after such an encounter. Such promotion is inherently evil in nature, and counterproductive to all involved; as an individual race, and humanity at large. The "Dominion" exploits this as it is an effective program to destroy humanity, and it is working. I should point out that no activity can be viewed as positive, when it comes to one race imposing unfair or immoral behavior toward another. Exploitation of this type of behavior is strictly not allowed. It does not matter which race conducts it or which race the behavior is directed against.

What can a black person do to achieve a more positive situation on Earth?

Chapter 11
The Races

All black people will be able to thrive better in a black community, with its own black only schools, places of worship, and businesses. I know this is against what is being put out by the "Dominion", with lots of propaganda behind it, however a quick check of the state of the black race in America in 1965, and comparisons with today will show the following: lower standard of actual knowledge from the education system, more strife, more crime, more immorality, elimination of a good cohesive, and supportive family. The results which stem from this so called "improved" lifestyle are self-evident. I am glad this question came up because this will demonstrate the love all Aldebaran's have for all of the races. Currently the "Dominion" opposes the black community with several propaganda campaigns like integration and government handouts.

Chapter 11
The Races

Additionally, think of this: Do races of people not cluster together naturally anyway? Diversity is good to certain extent, but with diversity comes enhanced animosity due to cultural differences. Do cats and dogs fight when together? Yes they do, unless they are taught by a superior being to get along. But until they are at that point then they will naturally fight to survive. The conflict is natural among races of people, but it is especially apparent among black communities that are impoverished and release their anger out on the people they perceive as their enemy. So they group together in tribal clusters just as all people do. Some of the safest places are the places where there are only people of like color/race. Yes, we do need to learn to get along, but people are different and will always have different beliefs. We should not expect Black people to behave as white people, just as

Chapter 11
The Races

we should not expect white people to behave as black people. We should love and care for all people, but the fact remains we are all different, and the conflict that the world experiences is simply a divergence of opinions

To fight this all of the Black Race should form campaigns which teach the following: Creation of and Maintaining a family structure, abandonment of social programs. Learn to stand on your own by refusing handouts, and earn every feature you have, this will strengthen your community more than you realize. Save up for, and create your own business areas.

Do not buy from other businesses unless you do not offer the product or service in your own community.

Immediately, stop all interracial breeding, dating, and marriage. Attend your own places of worship. Impose your own legal entity on your communities, including your own incarceration systems, absolutely demand good behavior, and high morals for members of your race, no matter where on the planet they may be located. Get as much education as you can, seek improvement, and form your own education system just for yourselves. Wipe out crime from the most petty to the most extreme in your race. If possible relocate as many persons as possible to black homelands. All of these things must be accomplished, or eventually the current "Dominion" system that has been emplaced (which is decaying the black race) will continue to destroy you from within. Someday, I sincerely hope, The Aldebaran Chime will be able to escort your ships, to your intended home world. This outcome will only happen if the changes can be made. You must realize that multiple times I, and I alone have spoken on behalf of the black race with the Administrators to prevent the elimination of this race.

Chapter 11
The Races

This is the reason this subject gets the attention that is placed upon it in this book.

Some of the information I have provided here seems harsh and may trigger accusations of racism based on "Dominion" propaganda schemes. I have noticed several upstarts in the Black Race who have begun to see through the "Dominion's" schemes. These upstarts should receive the support of all persons as they are on the correct spiritual and life-wave path.

Were Blacks once the fabled Egyptians?

No, this is more "Dominion" propaganda. This information was presented through some of the Black Race under "Dominion" control many years ago. Some current black leaders now parrot this doctrine. Careful investigation will easily reveal this is a false

Chapter 11
The Races

doctrine, and again providing the "Dominion" with an easy way to discredit some black scholars and leaders.

Having revealed this, I can say certain black people lived in Egypt from time to time. The original leaders and priests were from what we now call Sumeria, and were of the Aryan Race. Many leaders in Egypt listened to Chime and "The Aldebaran 33s" in those days, but corruption set in, and narcissisms took many over. The country declined into ruin, over many ups, and downs.

The Arabs

Arabs are currently in all manner of disarray due to a Dominion emplaced "requirement" to occupy lands not assigned to Arab peoples. This is an addition to the original texts, which were inserted at or near the origins of the religion (via a Dominion allied members

Chapter 11
The Races

of Mohammad's family). This requirement is effectively destroying the Arabic peoples, and was influenced by Dominion forces at that time, for an arrangement of "riches" passed to the scribes and family who were writing it, "what could just a few lines of writing do?", "so what, it is just a book." This has caused the Arabic speaking people's undue suffering and wastes their resources. A reconstruction of the previous religions of the areas will restore these people to their correct and right situation.

The Light skinned races fared better than other groups on the planet, as they maintained their own religions for a longer time. Even in the advance of other religions they maintained their own identity and can easily reconstruct the previous religions. Also the wave compatibility with the Chime played a role as well. In any case a recent wave of immigrants into the homelands of these peoples threatens destruction, and

Chapter 11
The Races

if the light skinned races fall so will the entire planet. This is seen as a huge play of the Dominion, and it has dire consequences for the entire species of mankind. All light skinned races should come together, purge the traitors, and reconnect in the light skinned native lands.

The races of the last group, which are in modern times considered darker skinned Chinese and pacific natives and others, are currently being led astray. All manner of sexual diseases, the development of "dark" religions, drug abuse, and perversions are cast in their societies by Dominion operatives. All of this must be stopped. Oppose all such activity, be active and do all you can to correct this imbalance.

Chapter 12:

Who am I?

1.3.0

Chapter 12

Who Am I?

I am known as 1.3.0. , (One Three Zero), a Chime classification system, used by "The Children of R". I live in a human and do have an everyday name, have a normal life, and live in a country on planet earth in a physical body at least for now. I am originally from Aldebaran.

My normal state is "Chime". I was sent with other "Chime" here as a group of 3. I am the only one of the 3 currently manifest in a physical body the other 2 passed back to "Chime" and remain in connection with me. They were both persecuted via the "Dominion" directly, until physical body death, one in the 1980s and one a few years ago. We have been here for several lifespans. Additionally the publisher suggested I use a penname so I chose "Ranald."

Upon completion of my tasks, (and if possible the completion of 2 other tasks) we will return fully as

Chapter 12

Who Am I?

a group (a Chime Triad). As "Chimes", we are never totally separate. Never!

Are you, the author, one of "The Children of R".

Yes, A Chime from the R solar system (Aldebaran)

Were you a part of the Remote Viewing program of the United States?

No, my "Chime Triad" was incorporated into another program, the RV program was to locate "things or information", and my group was entirely to cause change or phenomenon. I can say we were located somewhat in the same general area as the RV program, just not a part of it. It is notable that several of Maria's Vril friends, and helpers were also incorporated into this program which explains why it did not resurface in Germany after the war. The RV program was entirely human based, no Aldebaran's, or "Chime" were used in it. At the time I did know of the RV program, and I would venture to guess they knew of us. In either case the RV program is of no concern to me.

Are you a Prophet?

No

Are you a teacher?

Yes

Do you have a website?

Yes, the publisher has created a page for me. It can be found on TaijituHouse.com

Do you hate the "Dominion"?

No, I do not hate anyone.

Chapter 12

Who Am I?

Have you struggled or fought with the "Dominion" first hand?

Yes, many times. This opposition is required of me and will likely take the life of my physical body at some point.

Explain "Chime" :

"Chime" is another state of being beyond the wave format. All I can say is that you recognize a difference in material things, and something abstract for example music. This is the sort of situation here. For Earth Life-waves or humans, this is beyond the current ability of your understanding.

Chapter 13

Common Questions

Chapter 13

Common Questions

In this Chapter there are 37 of the most common questions I am asked and their answers. I hope this Chapter and the Glossary will clear up any questions you might have for me.

1. What about GMO foods?

This is a "Dominion" program. A very large program indeed! There has been quite a bit of research done on this since the 1940s by the "Dominion" forces. The seeds have been modified to give docility to the human race, to create health issues, to dwindle down the population, and to modify humans to make them more controllable. The GMO seeds are also more respondent to the chemical spraying methodology currently imposed on the entire planet as they will only grow if sprayed with toxic chemicals. Currently research is being done in Israel to program these seeds with all variety of modifications to the DNA strands with previous research having been done in South Africa (Mandela years included), US, France, Hungary,

Bulgaria, Romania (with involvement and support from the British royals), Latvia, Iraq (pre Saddam), Niger, Egypt, Turkey, Japan, Venezuela, Nicaragua, Canada, Australia, New Zealand, Saudi Arabia, and a few others to minor extents.

2. What are the "Dominion's" plans for the future of Mankind ?

The "Dominion" intends to take over and exercise total control. Their plan is to set up here on Earth and use this as a base to attack and destroy, Aldebaran. They want to rule the entire galaxy and then attack other galaxies. This is to say they want it all.

3. Are governments under control of the "Dominion"? Absolutely

Yes. All are to some degree. Some are worse than others. Some are more or less nearly neutral. This does not mean that the populations of those countries are "Dominion" supporting, usually the populations are not and unaware of what is truly happening in their country.

Chapter 13

Common Questions

The one country under the most control without any doubt is Israel, 95% and rising, followed up closely by Turkey, Saudi Arabia, Egypt, Iran, Afghanistan, and Great Britain, about 80-85%. It is growing in the United States, Lebanon, Iraq, India, Russia, Pakistan, the rest of continental Europe, all remaining Arabic speaking countries, China and India in the 70% range. All remaining countries except a very few are running in the 60% plus range. Nepal seems to be the current lowest at about 55%. Individual humans are as a whole, slightly tilted in the Dominion range. This can be reversed.

4. Are "The Children of R" doing anything to stop the "Dominion"?

Absolutely, every hour of every day, the "The Children of R" are attempting to ruin the "Dominion's" plans, make them less effective, or expose the "Dominion" activities to the public. The more light shined on the "Dominion" the more power they lose. The "Dominion" need the power they get from the public to succeed in their endeavors. The "Dominion" is well aware of the tactics being used against them, but to reveal actual active programs, and tactics is unwise to do so here.

Chapter 13

Common Questions

5. Is the Taliban, or Al Qaeda part of the "Dominion"?

Yes. Please note the organizations which give these groups power are also part of the "Dominion".

6. Was the hippie movement part of the "The Children of R"?

No, it was a part of the "Dominion", in its beginning.

"The Children of R" attempted to change it, and in doing so the "Dominion" removed power from it, and this in turn caused it to fade out. Please read, "Weird Scenes inside The Canyon", to clarify this.

7. Is the Illuminati evil?

The Illuminati is currently a buzz word for the under organizations of the "Dominion". Therefore in this sense, yes it is. A clever tactic of the "Dominion" is to basically steal names from "The Children of R". Many years ago the "The Children of R" used this name in the form of "Illume" (to shine light). The "Dominion" named a group after it the Illuminate', and it

Chapter 13

Common Questions

was geared to the infiltration of several human groups, and rendered them ineffective. To eliminate such confusion, occasionally the "The Children of R" have to change names, due to "Dominion" programs of disinformation.

8. Did Evil exist on Earth before the 'Dominion' arrived?

A very good question, the answer is somewhat complicated but, actually it did not. Nature is sometimes cruel in a way but not powered or driven by evil.

9. Can the 'Dominion' harm Chime?

No, they can only kill the humanoid body a Chime occupies. "Dominion" can do nothing at all to a "Chime" in "Chime" only state. Each Aldebaran Chime they manage to murder, discredit, or weaken the "Dominion" lose more, and more power, and the Aldebaran's gain power. This is why the "Dominion" prefers to mess with human life-waves. Mostly low level human Dominion sympathizers desire to kill a Chime in human bodies, and always to their own detriment.

Chapter 13

Common Questions

10. Are Chimes God?

No

11. When did Aldebaran's arrive?

Thousands of years ago. The most early intelligent civilizations of humans were established by the Aldebaran's. This is covered in a previous chapter.

12. Did the Aldebaran's create humans?

No, a previous group did, partly from existing beings on the planet. I refer to the creators as the "aliens". This might be a poor word choice on my behalf, since it creates imagery which is not true. In any case the "aliens" lost a war and retreated. A regulatory group was called in, "The Administrators", superior to the aliens. Two groups came to humanity and each represent each side of the war, but neither are the actual "aliens". One is "The Children of R" (from Aldebaran), and the other is the "Dominion". All this is covered in a previous chapter.

Chapter 13

Common Questions

13. What are UFOs?

They are human ships for the most part, which have been reverse engineered, or the plans for them have been given to the groups by the "Dominion". There are occasional ships from Aldebaran, and the "Dominion" home world that are allowed by "The Administrators", but they are really huge, and also small supply ships exist. There are bases on moons, and planets by all sides, and there are "Administrator" owned robotic vessels as well. Most governments are aware of the Aldebaran ship which flies very close to the surface of the Sun at all times. A similar "Dominion" Ship stays just past Saturn.

14. Are Gays/Lesbians Evil?

Again, I cover this material in the text, but this depends upon the course they decide to take.

15. Why is being Gay/Lesbian of Dominion?

This is a good question, a tough one considering the Dominion's massive propaganda, but I will leave it at the fact, it diminishes the Life-Wave of humans. It weakens them to certain dissolvement of the life wave.

Chapter 13

Common Questions

16. Do animals go to the next realm?

Yes

17. Do animals have a Life-wave?

Yes, it is different than human Life-wave though.

Please note: Zoophilia or Bestiality is another way to cancel out your life-wave as the wavelengths are not compatible for mating purposes.

18. Is the Law of Attraction for Real?

Yes, the law of attraction is real.

19. Why does the Law of Attraction sometimes not work?

Basically there are a few reasons, the want of something too specific, the want of something contrary to the Universe/Humans/Race/Individuals. Having a want, and not taking any activities to help it come to fruition, and want without any definition of what the want is, cancels out the attraction.

Chapter 13

20. Are all Wars bad?

Yes, all wars are bad.

21. Is area 51 a place of Evil?

In the sense that the "Dominion" have humans working for them there, Yes.

22. Are Secret Societies Evil?

Some are some are not. Either way most are ineffective. Ones which are currently significant are usually political influencing in nature.

23. Are there documents hidden in Egypt/Sumeria/ Jundi Shappur/Oak Island/Languedoc (et al) which are significant to humankind?

Yes, the "Dominion" seems to be able to fund expeditions to confiscate such documentation, and either destroy it, or hide it away. The old adage, seek, and find is the technique. Humankind need to develop on this subject, and publish it immediately after finding before the "Dominion" can manipulate the truth.

24. Did the "Dominion" or "Dominion" controlled forces kill US President J.F. Kennedy?

Yes, "Dominion" controlled forces killed JFK.

25. Are people powerless to oppose the "Dominion"?

Absolutely Not! The "Dominion" here, can be defeated by Humans, if so desired.

26. Why does the "Dominion" want to destroy humans?

To gain power, perceived influence, to take the planet, and use remaining humans as slaves or food.

27. Can people use Dowsing Rods/Cast or Throw Stones/Pendulums/Tarot to help with ordinary day to day situations?

Yes

Chapter 13
Common Questions

28. What about the legend of the crystal skulls?

A "Dominion" hoax.

29. How much longer will Humanity live/last?

It depends upon Humanity and the progress made, if continuing on the current path, not long.

30. Are Spirit Guides for Real?

Yes, to the extent that they are Non-corporeal beings. Some may have their own agenda. I say for each person to exercise caution. Some work for the "Dominion," Especially if the human is working for the "Dominion". The reality is you do not need them at all. You have what you need all along inside yourself.

31. Are Fairies, Leprechauns, Sprites, and other Mythical Beings real?

Yes, some are quite real Nature Spirits, and some are hoaxes. The real ones are non-corporeal beings.

Many are simple beings, and many can be seen in certain conditions.

Chapter 13

Common Questions

32. Are such creatures evil?

No, most are not

33. Are "Chime" Infallible?

No, wisdom is common to all "Chime", actually all "Chime" have an aspect of being which is an interconnectedness to all other "Chime". The "giving up of secrets" is sort of a buzzword for becoming "Chime."

"Chime" is a state of existence, compatible with all of the Aldebaran's, and the light skinned races of earth human's lifeforms. All "Chime" can, and have made mistakes. The Aldebaran's are a very peaceful, and mild race, and their "Chime" is even milder.

34. Are the British Royals part of the "Dominion's" human supporters?

Yes

35. Are some aliens reptilians?

Yes, or at least to humans they resemble reptilians.

Chapter 13

Common Questions

There are several very different groups which humans would call reptilian. It is notable that one group of these races is a sort of priest class in the galaxy; meaning that they are very empathetic, and serve as counsellors, and judges. I am limited to the information I can give on this matter.

36. Are some aliens insects?

No, not earth type insects, but some aliens do resemble (in some ways) insect type bodies. Again there are varieties of aliens which humans would refer to them as insect like. Some are "Dominion" allied, and some are not.

37. What are the correct Religions?

Each variety of Human Life-wave was provided an original religion on Earth. This is what I mean by correct. Perhaps this is better shown in examples.

Example A :
A man living in Iran is a Shia Muslim but can sense this religion is not exactly right for him. I would say to this man research, and you will find that before Islam came to Iran, there were

other religions that practiced there. I would advise him to research into these religions, and he will find the one which resonates with his Life-wave.

Example B :

A woman living in Germany finds that Catholic Christianity does not resonate with her Life-wave. Again I advise her to look into the ancient people's religion of that area, and one will be found which does resonate with her Life-wave. I hope this clears up the issue of correct religion.

"Resist the propaganda, be strong, be compassionate, but most importantly: expose the lies to weaken the enemy."

With all the love a Chime can convey,

I.3.0

THE CHILDREN OF R:

"Plans from Beyond the Earth Plane"

I.3.0

Ranald

Glossary of Terms and Related Definitions

Glossary of Terms and Related Definitions

Aldebaran 33

A limit of 33 Chime stationed on Earth to influence the outcome of the Earth Lifewave to enter into the galaxy's Council of Aliens, now being replaced by Earth 33 humans.

Aldebaran Lifewave

A race, living on Aldebaran, with corporeal bodies which are very similar to some Earth Lifewave bodies. These Lifewaves may become Chime due to the constant contact with them upon their death and this is an aspiration of most Aldebaran Citizens. Aldebaran Lifewaves are modified in a way that they can constantly communicate with those that are Chime.

Arab

These are peoples inhabiting the area in and around the Arabian Peninsula, but no further.

Caucasian/North Oriental/Aryan

The light skinned races originally occupying Europe through Northern Asia, to the Korean Peninsula and Japanese islands. This encompasses all Caucasian peoples, in many sub races. These are Germans, Nordics, Slavs, Mongolians, Russians, Koreans and Japanese, some Persians, some Indians and the northern Chinese.

Chime

A Higher Form Life-wave, living on Aldebaran in non-corporeal form. Beloved by Aldebaran's, Chime are created in groups of three, as perceived by humans-one male and two

Glossary of Terms and Related Definitions

females (one "female" is actually sort of androgyny and is the leader of the Chime Triad). These will in turn procreate more Chime, but on a span of millions of years. Some select Aldebaran Life-waves "convert" into Chime upon death and organize into the system of threes as well. The Chime state is beyond what is called a "Mathematical being", which is matter and antimatter.

Controlling Alien

A group which lost the Great Alien Wars of the Galaxy, the remnants of which are now allied with the Dominion.

Human Lifewave

The Earth Human is a Lifewave made from the Genetic Modifier Aliens out of life waves from early earth, their own race and some from other planets. One is the Mud Planet of which the majority of earth human wave and genetic material came from. There were several races developed and only four races are left today of any noticeable size of population.

Negroid

This group occupied Africa southward of the Sahara and across some islands and into Australia. This group has an incompatible Lifewave with any other group on Earth. This Lifewave group was created to mine gems and minerals for the Genetic Modifier Aliens on another planet which has conditions of which their bodies are adapted. These people were modified on Earth for an eventual move to the planet before the Aliens were defeated.

Glossary of Terms and Related Definitions

Ranald

A penname that was selected per request of the publisher

Southern Oriental/Trans Pacific Natives/ American Natives

These peoples include a variety of sub races, from Southern Chinese, to island peoples across the Pacific, and southward into the Thailand area and on the Malaysian peninsula. They are darker skinned people, but not negroid.

The Administrators

The Galaxy has a powerful group of Entities "The Administrators" who control the Galaxy, these are well beyond the ability to become controlled by any other entity or Lifewave. The Administrators role on Earth: Beings beyond Lifewave which are assigned to protect the Galaxy. They do not generally interfere or participate in Lifewave activity. The Galactic War necessitated involvement in several specific places, one being Earth. A decision will be made to either admit Earth to the Galactic Council or destroy it, based upon the progress of two groups assigned there.

The Allies (Galatic Council)

A group of aliens opposing the Dominion.

Glossary of Terms and Related Definitions

The Council of Aldebaran

This is the governing body of Aldebaran, currently the council is in charge of the Children of R and Earth 33,on Earth as well. The Council has both Aldebaran people and Chime, as members of The Council. Aldebaran is a Earth name for the solar system called by it's inhabitants, "R".

The Dominion

A powerful group of Lifewaves with self-interest and exploitation as their primary features. The Dominion 99 – A group limited to 33, but later multiplied by 3 to form 99 positions with a tradeoff of division of power to 30% each, a total of 9% was given up for this move. This group also wants to influence of the Earth Lifewaves to become slaves for the Dominion. Currently they promote self interest in traitorous Human Lifewave for control.

The Dominion 99

A group limited to 33, but multiplied by 3 to form 99 positions with a tradeoff of division of power to 30% each, a total of 9% was given up for this move. This group also wants to influence of the Earth Lifewaves to become slaves for the Dominion. Currently they promote self interest in traitorous Human Lifewave for control.

The Genetic Modifier Aliens

Glossary of Terms and Related Definitions

The aliens who created the original Human Lifewave forms. They are now defeated and small in number. They were allied with the Dissenting Aliens of the Galaxy, now defeated. These appear to humans as a frog-like being. To create a genetic modified being, one of their own, loses it's life. The genetic modifiers operate from naturally evolved methods to accomplish the task.

Earth 33

A group of 33 people, from the light skinned races, each an earth native, selected by the Chime and the Galactic Council, and to whom, the title transferred, is no longer just an Earth Life-wave. They can become Aldebaran citizens, just like Maria Ortisch did. They are all eligible to become "Chime" themselves someday just as Maria did. Each has a responsibility to produce Dominion retraction from Earth.

The Shining Ones on Aldebaran

Chime, who formerly have served one or more human lives on Earth

In loving dedication to my Eun and Elaine, human

manifestations of Chime Triad 1.3.0.

1.3.0.

Maria

Bis später!

www.the33.org

OTHER TAIJITU HOUSE TITLES

Books

The Book of Powers, by A.J. Christoph

The Search for the Hidden Door, Marshall N. Lever

We hope you enjoyed this *Taijitu House* book. For more information on authors, titles, and author events please visit our website at:

WWW.TAIJITUHOUSE.COM

www.ingramcontent.com/pod-product-compliance
Lightning Source LLC
Chambersburg PA
CBHW071940090426
42740CB00011B/1760